Faiths in Green

Religious Ethics and Environmental Challenges

Series Editors: Sarah E. Fredericks, University of Chicago; Kevin J. O'Brien, Pacific Lutheran University

Advisory Board

Dianna Bell, Evan Berry, Willis Jenkins, James Miller, Kyle Powys White, and Whitney Sanford

Religion shapes human responses to twenty-first-century environmental challenges—discouraging some adherents from accepting scientific evidence, encouraging others to make sacrifices to preserve ecosystems, and leading still others to develop new spiritual traditions. This interdisciplinary series explores the ways diverse religious communities can, should, and do respond to contemporary environmental challenges. Many of the works will be explicitly ethical, dealing with normative commitments, applied ethics, or ethical theory; others will be theological or philosophical; still others may be social scientific descriptions. Since readers of the series will come from diverse academic contexts, all works will be explicit about methodology, enabling conversation across disciplines. We are particularly interested in works that (1) bring together distinct branches of scholarship to address practical or theoretical issues that cannot be addressed by one alone (e.g., linking healthcare ethics and environmental ethics or comparing religious traditions); (2) explore under-researched religious communities, subcommunities, and traditions; or (3) investigate commonly studied religions in a novel way. We welcome monographs, edited volumes, and exemplary revised dissertations that take one of these approaches. While not all works in the series need to be normative or contemporary, all will help readers advance conversations about the ways religion aids or hinders responses to contemporary environmental challenges.

Titles in the Series

Faiths in Green: Religion, Environmental Change, and Environmental Concern in the United States, by Lukas Szrot

Gratitude for the Wild: Christian Ethics in the Wilderness, by Nathaniel James Van Yperen

Redeeming Sin? Social Diagnostics amid Ecological Destruction, by Ernst M. Conradie

Theological and Ethical Perspectives on Climate Engineering: Calming the Storm, edited by Forrest Clingerman and Kevin J. O'Brien

Faiths in Green

Religion, Environmental Change, and Environmental Concern in the United States

Lukas Szrot

LEXINGTON BOOKS

Lanham • Boulder • New York • London

Published by Lexington Books
An imprint of The Rowman & Littlefield Publishing Group, Inc.
4501 Forbes Boulevard, Suite 200, Lanham, Maryland 20706
www.rowman.com

6 Tinworth Street, London SE11 5AL, United Kingdom

British Library Cataloguing in Publication Information Available

Library of Congress Cataloging-in-Publication Data

Names: Szrot, Lukas, author.
Title: Faiths in green : religion, environmental change, and environmental concern in the
    United States / Lukas Szrot.
Description: Lanham, Maryland : Lexington Books, [2021] | Series: Religious ethics and
    environmental challenges | Includes bibliographical references and index.
Identifiers: LCCN 2021006358 (print) | LCCN 2021006359 (ebook) |
    ISBN 9781793630124 (cloth) | ISBN 9781793630131 (epub) |
    ISBN 9781793630148 (pbk)
Subjects: LCSH: Environmentalism—United States—History. | Environmentalism—
    United States—Religious aspects.
Classification: LCC GE197 .S97 2021 (print) | LCC GE197 (ebook) |
    DDC 201/.77—dc23
LC record available at https://lccn.loc.gov/2021006358
LC ebook record available at https://lccn.loc.gov/2021006359

∞™ The paper used in this publication meets the minimum requirements of American
National Standard for Information Sciences—Permanence of Paper for Printed Library
Materials, ANSI/NISO Z39.48-1992.

Dedication
To my niece and nephews
Kylie, Darrien, Kyler, and Kason
The children of the future, and of generations to come

Contents

Acknowledgments

Though the research project on which this work is based yielded a completed and successfully defended PhD dissertation, as well as parts of several narrowly focused empirical articles aimed at an academic audience (some of which are still underway), the purpose of this book is not to earn a degree or add to a specialist literature so much as to tell a story. This is a story about both *how* and *why* these changes in U.S.-Americans' perceptions of the environment have occurred, what they mean in the context of present and future environmental change (some would say impending environmental *catastrophe*), and some of the inspiration behind the work. Though this story is loosely based on research conducted between January 2016 and April 2019, it is part of a lifelong effort to better understand the relationships between societies and nature. I write this story from the North Woods of Minnesota, a far cry from a childhood in North Texas or early professional life in Northeast Kansas, knowing there is always more to be done.

Writing is often a solitary endeavor, and I tend to value the solitude that comes with it, but like all else that is human, it is also a cooperative, social effort from beginning to end. Though I am by training a sociologist, this work would not have been possible without interdisciplinary mentorship and inspiration within the university environment, as well as a lot of support from outside it. I am particularly grateful to my mentors and advisors. First, my dissertation co-chairs: sociologist Robert J. Antonio and sociologist/gerontologist David Ekerdt. I became inspired by the former to look more closely at the U.S.-American pragmatist tradition, as well as some of the trends in U.S.-American politics, that have shaped both environmental issues and religion, past and present. From the latter, I learned how to think through measuring change over time from multiple different angles, and how to explain methods and findings in clear and accessible terms. From both, I learned how to be a more effective scholar, as well as a more authentic and conscientious human being (though I, like the lifelong effort the story is part of, remain very much a work in progress!). This book never would have been possible without them.

Additionally, Ebenezer Obadare, a sociologist and international relations scholar, helped me think through how to do the hard-hitting, multidimensional empirical work demanded by sociology, while also staying true to my early academic background as a philosopher of religion, morality, and knowledge. We had some great conversations over breakfast and coffee. Paul V. Stock, a sociologist and environmental studies scholar, offered guidance on how to keep real-life personhood centrally relevant in a "big-data"-driven research project like this one. It was an honor to collaborate on a book chapter on food justice, and it was inspiring thinking through how people can better relate to the natural world, and to one another. Lesa Hoffman, an expert in quantitative methodology in education and the behavioral sciences, trained me in the systematic analysis and presentation of data; without her guidance (and encouragement to get the "done kind" of dissertation) this project would not have been possible. Experimental physicist Alice Bean kept me honest when it came to data analysis and reporting error in prediction and trajectory. I am grateful for your information and insights on climate change communication with faith-based communities from your work with the U.S. State Department, which you shared with me as I worked through this project. I still have much to learn, in all these regards.

Thank you to my wife Charline, for sticking by me through over two decades of a wonderful relationship, including the eleven years I've spent in college during that time. I have always been a dreamer. Sometimes dreams come true. But it cannot have been easy. I'd also like to thank our dog Chewie, who rescued us back in 2015 and has become an integral part of our daily lives. Much of what is written here found its way into my conscious mind during our long walks together. My parents, Lou and Cindy, have always been supportive of my desire (compulsion?) to write, since I wrote that first story on a notepad with a pencil over three decades ago (thanks Dad!). My sister Katie and my extended family, too, as well as the long trail of friendships that I've been honored to be a part of over the decades (even if some of those trails have since gone a bit cold through neglect)—along the way, I hope to have written something loved ones and friends will pick up and enjoy.

My colleagues at Bemidji State University—particularly Rucha Ambikar, Colleen Greer, Donna Pawlowski, John Perlich, and Debra Peterson of the Sociology, Anthropology, and Communication Studies Department—have been wonderfully supportive during my transition to assistant professorship, and I hope that we will collaborate on future projects (as I write, we already are!). It has also been a welcome chance to think about science education and crunch numbers again on a project I have been working on with Katie

Peterson from the Department of Chemistry. I truly feel welcome at Bemidji State. I appreciate the many brilliant students I have met along the way at the universities at which I have taught, and learned, though I am afraid a list would be too long, and I would inevitably leave too many out. And indeed, none of this would have been possible without the support of my mentor and friend, Ben Agger (1952–2015), University of Texas at Arlington. You are dearly missed. I also benefited from the guidance and knowledge of Heather Jacobson, Beth Anne Shelton, Jason E. Shelton, Robert Kunovich, Emily Rauscher, Eric Hanley, ChangHwan Kim, Mehrangiz Najafizedeh, Kelly Chong, Brian Donovan, David Norman Smith, Kevin McCannon, Lisa-Marie Wright, David Arditi, Bob Young, M. Faye Hanson-Evans, Dorothy Kalanzi, Raymond Eve, Linda Rouse, Tim Luke, and Christopher T. Conner (among many others) during my years in graduate study and early academic life.

I would also like to thank those environmental researchers, sociologists of religion, and other voices of encouragement who have been instrumental in helping me keep this project moving forward. In particular, friends and fellow travelers in environmental sociology Matt Comi and Brock Ternes, with whom I am collaborating on works in progress, and Nathan R. Collins, with whom I have successfully collaborated in the past. I also appreciate scholarly guidance and examples of Gregory Cushman, David Fowle, and Joseph Brewer at the University of Kansas Environmental Studies Department; Elaine Howard Ecklund (Rice University) and John H. Evans (University of California, San Diego) of the Network for the Social Scientific Study of Religion and Science; and John Grim and Mary Evelyn Tucker at the Yale School of the Environment. I would also like to thank a new friend and colleague Randhir Gautam for the recent opportunity to speak to students and faculty on environmental justice at Raffles University, Neemrana, India. Finally, I am grateful to anyone who is reading this sentence—you have taken the time to pick up this work. I hope this will be one of many.

Lukas Szrot, PhD
Assistant Professor of Sociology
Bemidji State University

Chapter 1

Sacred Places in a Risk Society

For the first seven years of my life, my family moved around a lot, before finally settling in a bustling suburb in North Texas. Growing up there, I must've spent thousands of hours in the park nearby, where a massive, gnarled old tree stood like a lone sentinel in the center of a sprawling meadow. Over time, that tree became a sort of sacred place, where I could think, muse, and clear my head. When my wife and I moved into an apartment near that park years later, I resumed my trips to that old tree for introspection. It must have been at least a century old, enduring dozens of droughts, lightning strikes, and tornado-producing storms. In the first decades of my life, that old tree came to symbolize weathering profound, widespread, and sometimes cataclysmic change.

The last time I visited that old tree, only a stump remained, cut low to the ground. The surrounding grass had turned from a verdant green to the color of dry straw, sprouting through crisscrossing cracks in the parched earth. The wildflowers at the periphery were gone. It was hotter and drier than it had once been. Water was in shorter supply, and that old tree, a solitary watchtower that stood through the decades and their attendant vicissitudes, was dead. I told myself that it was "just a tree," that it was old, that things changed . . . but that did little to assuage a real and nagging sense of loss.

It took decades for those environmental changes to happen, but they have become increasingly difficult to ignore. I wonder how many others had grown up to watch old trees die and get cut down, how many other beds of wildflowers had been mowed over, how much wild grass and underbrush had turned from green to yellow-brown. Through reading, studying, and paying attention to current events, other environmental changes with more dire human impacts became tragically clear: people evacuating coastal residences in the face of rising tides, or washed out to sea by stronger storm surges. How many have lost homes, workplaces, schools, and even loved ones to environmental change? I also began to wonder about others who lived life outside: farmers watching crops succumb to increasingly frequent droughts and floods, outdoor aficionados witnessing green spaces withering, lakes and rivers growing stagnant, dry, or dead, populations of native animal species plummeting as invasive species multiplied unchecked.

Environments are changing. Those who spend enough time outside can *see* it happening. In many ways, scientists continue to confirm on a global scale what can be witnessed on the ground with increasing clarity. This is not a scholarly treatise on environmental science, though I do draw on a range of scientific findings and insights. It is (mostly) not a jeremiad about human despoliation of the environment, either. It is an effort to describe, and explain, *perceptions* of environmental change, and how they are related to religion and the sacred, past and present: *how, and why, have these perceptions changed?* For environments, change can happen gradually, or in catastrophic bursts. For people, change over time occurs in three ways: changes over individual people's lifetimes, changes across generations, and changes, year by year. All three kinds of change are included in this work, but I focus mostly on the first and second, for reasons I'll get into later. Between early 2016 and the present, I combed through history, theory, and data gathered by the General Social Survey (Smith et al. 2015), examining how people perceive environmental change, or *environmental concern,* across those born between 1884 and 1996. Sometimes, I go back a bit further to try to make sense of things historically, or draw on theory along with a few personal anecdotes.

It was painful to witness the death of that old tree, but my mourning, I am sure, pales compared to some of the other impacts of environmental changes already underway, as well as those to come. Though I like to spend unstructured time outside, I'm trained as a sociologist. What, then, can sociology offer in terms of *bearing witness* or of *coming to terms with* these changes? Every story needs to set the scene somehow, and there are three ways I do so in this chapter. The first involves thinking about environmental change *sociologically,* connecting the human and the nonhuman worlds. The second involves re-thinking assumptions about religion and the sacred. Third, I address the importance of *change over time,* including how to think about religion as a social phenomenon shaped over time by ongoing interaction between people, institutions, and the broader culture of which it is part.

WHEN SALESPEOPLE BECOME GIANT INSECTS

First, a metaphor appropriate to the scale and scope of environmental change: sociologist Ulrich Beck provided a promising term in the form of *Die*

Verwandlung (Beck 2015, 75). This German term translates roughly to "the metamorphosis." It was chosen deliberately to reflect both Beck's influence and the work *Die Verwandlung* by author Franz Kafka which influenced him in turn. In Kafka's work, which inspired multiple films in the twentieth century, a salesman awakens to find that he has been transformed into a giant insect. Environmental change turns sacred spaces into proto-deserts, coastal domiciles into imperiled shorefronts, or plentiful fauna into endangered species. With Beck (2015), I maintain that environmental change *is;* it exists, and is happening, regardless of how people *think about it.* I take the reality of environmental change for granted, but the ways that people think about these changes (or don't) are far from irrelevant. Part of the moral of Kafka's tale, and part of Beck's thesis, involves *coming to terms with a new reality*—a brand new, fundamentally different, unnerving sort of reality, a "new modernity" (see also Beck 1992). *Coming to terms* means a process of making sense—in this case, making sense of how attitudes toward the environment have changed *over time.* Though I am not the first to look to religion to explain this connection, religion is a part of the connection between people and environmental change, and is a part that involves a lot of *ambivalence* and *complexity* (see, for example, Gerten et al. 2018; Vaidyanathan et al. 2018). More on this in the next chapter.

Making this connection—between people and environments, *via* religion—can be difficult, because it is also an act of translation, part of a centuries-old, contentious effort to build bridges between science and the humanities (see Gould 2011). Having to speak the language of both art and science, both "subjective" impression and "objective" truth, sociologists may be especially well-positioned to aid with such translation work (Szrot 2015, 99–123). Speaking the language of science, human activity has affected environments for millennia. Conversations in the natural sciences have long involved debates as to when, and to what extent, a new era characterized by this human activity, the *Anthropocene*, began. A new word to *come to terms* with a new reality: human activity is the main driver in environmental changes so rapid and widespread that they mark a new era on the planet earth (Barnosky 2008; Crutzen 2002; Ellis et al. 2015; Kolbert 2014; Ruddiman 2003; Ruddiman et al. 2015). Environmental change is taking place on a scale, and at a rate, never witnessed by human beings before, and the main reason for this change is human activity. It is a truly profound metamorphosis, with impacts that have permanently reshaped the planet at virtually every level. As a sociologist, *coming to terms* means trying to better understand how people are making sense of this new reality through their interactions with one another, as well as interactions with the institutions they build and inhabit. In other words, the relationship between people and nature is built through ongoing understandings of what it means to be human, in ways that go beyond scientific findings and public (mis)perceptions of them. It is not enough to point to the trends; the real work lies in explaining them and in using them to tell a meaningful story. Understanding how people and nature, as well as science and storytelling, may be reconciled is part of *Die Verwandlung*.

Risk and Wickedness: A Moral Issue

Aside from clever insect–salesman metaphors, Beck (1992) was also widely known as a pioneer in the *sociology of risk*; his work focused on the role that scientific and technological development has played in creating new hazards, especially (but not only) environmental ones. In parallel, Giddens (2000) referred to a *runaway world*, a period of major historical transition affecting nearly every part of the planet in myriad ways (Giddens 2000, 19–20; see also Giddens 1990). The world is without doubt more interconnected than ever before, but the side effects of constant, accelerating, and ongoing change have created new social impacts, and hazards, with which human beings now struggle. Among these novel hazards is how societies affect, and are affected by, environmental change. The responses to such changes are often referred to as *environmental concern* (see Dunlap and Jones 2002).

Ironically, the Enlightenment promise that reason and science would lead to greater human ability to shape the future has birthed a world in which science and technology have discovered, and even created, new risks and uncertainties. These hazards and the changes that lead to them, *are*—they *exist*—and denizens of this "risk society" (for Beck), this "runaway world" (for Giddens), must come to terms with them. Here, the U.S. makes for an especially interesting case study. As concerns over environmental change have mounted globally, the U.S. remains one of the biggest drivers of such change (Stocker and Quin 2013). Critics have argued that the U.S. has gone from "a leader to a laggard" (Christoff and Eckersley 2013, 169) on environmental issues, exemplified recently in plans to withdraw from the Paris Agreement, a nonbinding global resolution to address global warming. As I wrote this book, the U.S. was the only signatory nation on earth to currently express this intent, and as I complete it, the impacts and future of this and other global environmental governance efforts are uncertain (BBC 2019; see also Holmes 2017; Meyer 2017). There are many ways to come to terms with *Die Verwandlung*, some riskier than others.

Environmental sociology is the ongoing effort to make sense of the connection between people and nature, especially the problems raised by environmental change. Environmental sociologists often do not walk the halls of power in the U.S., which may afford some freedom to speak truth to power (see Lidskog et al. 2015). This has often meant implicating the capitalist "economic growth imperative" as the primary cause of climate change, extinction of species, and an earth system generally overtaxed and "used unsustainably" by human beings (Antonio 2009; Antonio and Brulle 2011; Buttel 2004; Curran 2017; Daly 1996; Foster 1999; Klein 2014; Rosa et al. 2015; York and Rosa 2003). It follows that the global economic system needs to be changed if there is any hope of addressing environmental change in a lasting, effective, and equitable way. However, such change is strongly resisted by a powerful cadre of political actors and interests, funded in part by fossil fuel money, who cast doubt on the reality or risks of environmental change. Ongoing efforts to sow doubt about climate change, as well as other environmental and public health hazards, are made credible in part by Cold War fears that such talk is evidence of a creeping communist takeover and a threat to the U.S.-American way of life (Dunlap and McCright 2015; Oreskes and Conway 2010).

I don't dispute the value of honestly thinking about whether infinite economic growth is possible on a finite planet, or what role funding and politics play in research agendas and public opinion. However, I am convinced that is only part of the story. *Die Verwandlung*, environmental-change-as-metamorphosis, is both real and increasingly difficult to ignore. A problem that is real can only be denied for so long before it resists efforts to ignore or redefine it. I can hold my hand over a roaring fire and deny that it is hot for a few moments, but eventually it will burn me regardless of my opinions. As with Kafka's salesman, I will eventually have to come to terms with a new reality. Absent from that park in North Texas for years, I did not witness on a regular basis the land drying out, or the trees, grass, and flowers dying—but that did not make those changes any less clear when I returned.

Sadly, the impacts of human-driven environmental change are shared quite unevenly, having already "trickled down" to those least responsible for them (see Harlan et al. 2015). This kind of socially structured denial can also only last for so long. As Beck (1992) clarified nearly three decades ago, over time, risks also "trickle up" to impact people in ways that are not strictly determined by income, political power, social status, or geographic location (22–4). The bag of frozen broccoli I steamed and ate for dinner was likely grown in another part of the world, perhaps somewhere in Latin America or South America. Growers may have been exposed to pesticides that may have serious unintended consequences on their own long-term health, and the health of their families. Consequences, intended or not, may visit themselves on the human beings who made my dinner possible and the networks of people they are connected to, as well as surrounding plants and animals in those ecosystems, for years to come. Here in my apartment in Northern Minnesota, I may have ingested a tiny amount of said pesticide in my broccoli; it may have been shown to be safe by the best available information at present, but I, like the farmers who grew it, may learn someday that the "risk" associated with said pesticide was, over the long term, underestimated. Such thoughts will keep you awake if you let them, and that's just frozen broccoli.

When complex problems involving human decision-making arise, the way a problem is defined shapes the kinds of solutions people are willing to entertain. If *risk society* is increasingly the field on which environmental change takes place, then *wicked problems* can be thought of as the collections of risk that arise, and *wicked conflicts* are the result of human efforts to grapple with them. A *wicked problem* is a problem that involves profound complexity and uncertainty. When people are not sure what is happening, they tend to come up with all kinds of different definitions of what's going on. There probably is no single "correct" solution to a wicked problem, partly because there isn't wide agreement on how to define the problem, or even how serious a problem it is (see Balint et al. 2011; Rittel and Webber 1973). Efforts to define, and redefine, *wicked problems* lead to *wicked conflicts*. In studying conflicts surrounding land and wildlife in the Yellowstone National Park area, sociologist Justin Farrell (2015) argued that *wicked conflicts* seem impossible to solve, and keep coming back, because they involve conflicting definitions of what's happening. The conflicts, and how the problems that create them are defined, ultimately aren't about what's true or false, but are shaped by perceptions of what is good or bad, what is right or wrong. In other words, how people define or express concern over environmental change—*environmental concern*—is ultimately a *moral* issue.

Ongoing moral, cultural, and political conflicts are the inevitable byproducts of risk society, because the problems faced by such a society, and the conflicts that arise, are increasingly *wicked*. Understanding these kinds of problems means looking more closely at the social contexts in which actions are framed as right and wrong. If it is true that people can, and do, witness environmental change in their own backyards, then *how* do people come to terms with environmental change, and *why* do people hold various, and conflicting, views of environmental change? People's ideas about the environment come from many different sources. But people are likely to *think about* and *talk about* their moral views in specific ways, based on specific people and places that influence what they take to be good and bad, right and wrong. I submit that *religion* specifically, and *the sacred* generally, is an important part of understanding the moral dimensions of environmental change, as well as many other aspects of cultural and social life.

ISN'T RELIGION GOING AWAY?

According to theologian Harvey Cox, the word *secular* comes from the Latin *saeculum,* which means "present age" (Cox 1966, 16). The word *modern* also, literally, means *now-ness* (root *mode*). It's right there in the words: to be modern is to be secular, and secular, modern. In sociology of religion, *secularization theory*, broadly speaking, offers an affirmative answer to the deceptively simple question: is religion going away? Comparing a religious past to a secular present (with degrees of celebration or mourning depending on who is doing the comparing) is hardly a new idea, but it is one that shaped sociology from its roots. In early nineteenth-century France, Auguste Comte, the first person to use the term *sociology* in writing, expected societies to progress from a theological (or fictitious) stage, through a metaphysical (or philosophical) stage and into a final positive (or scientific) stage (see Lenzer 1998). Max Weber also famously analyzed how capitalism in modern life came from specific currents of Reformed Protestantism. He concluded that once these new arrangements were in place, concern for material gain overshadowed religious faith, which became a vestige of the past (Weber 2011, 177). The work ethic, and cultural currents, that came from Reformed Protestantism, ultimately doomed it: once industrial capitalist modernity came to be, their religious foundations were no longer needed.

For Comte, the growth of systematic scientific knowledge undermined religious truth; for Weber, work as a sacred calling took on the "character of sport" (Weber 2011, 177) as pursuit of profit and technical mastery came to undermine religious values. And as a sociologist of religion Christian Smith quipped ironically, "Why study something that is dying? It's like studying dinosaurs. It doesn't matter" (Smith 2014, 151). In sociology, secularization has taken on the character of an *axiom:* water is wet, triangles have three sides, and religion is going away. But there are really two parts to this axiom: what *is* and what *ought (not) to be.* On one hand, secularization is said to *describe* what *is:* religion is in decline, and has been for a while. There may be many reasons given for this decline (for Comte, science displaces religion; for Weber, capitalism makes it obsolete—these are two popular possibilities), but it is assumed to be terminal in any case. Sometimes, secularization takes on the character of a *norm,* or what *ought to be.* This line of argument, again for various reasons, suggests that without religion, people can, and *will,* come to see the world more clearly. Both aspects of the secularization axiom may conspire to lead some scholars to dismiss religion as an important piece of this puzzle, as well as many others. This may be especially true for scholars who are not themselves religious, and who wish that religion did not have the social impact that it often does.

There are good grounds on which to more closely examine both assumptions. The *descriptive* aspect of the secularization axiom reflects its Protestant, and Eurocentric, heritage. Beck, too, claimed that just as Protestant modernity liberated people from the benighted arms of medieval Catholicism, this "new modernity" has given rise to a new and anxious kind of individualism

(Beck 1992, 14). This individualism is built on the ruins of tradition: "God departed (or we displaced him). The word 'belief,' which once meant 'having experienced,' has taken on the rather shabby tones of 'against our better judgment'" (Beck 1992, 113). Beck's theory begins by dividing history into *pre-modern, modern,* and *reflexive modern* stages (Beck 1992, 2–3). This reflects a tendency among European and American social theorists to tell a version of a story, a *conjectural history* (Palmeri 2016, 1–16), or a "grand narrative" (Lyotard 1985) that "progresses" from a past "Dark Age" to a more enlightened present. In this story, both modern institutions and modern problems are constituted against, and shaped by, a background of inevitable and terminal religious decline.

Scientifically speaking, religion is likely not going away any time soon. Sociology of religion can be addressed in a single question and answer. *Is the world becoming more, or less, religious? Yes.* Norris and Inglehart (2011) offered a "demographic hypothesis" which fits the evidence nicely. In terms of *raw numbers*, there are more openly religiously unaffiliated human beings alive today than there have ever been. They can mostly be found in the wealthier parts of the world: Europe, Canada, Australia, and to some extent, the U.S. However, there has actually been a decline in the *percentage* of the world population which claims no religious affiliation (234). Partly this is because the fertility rates among religious persons are higher than those among the unaffiliated. Religious people are more likely to have children, and more likely to have more children (231–9). Among the strongest predictors of whether or not a person is religious is how they were raised (Pearce and Denton 2011, 23–4; Smith and Denton 2005; Smith and Snell 2009, 246–8). Even among academic scientists, probably the least religious subset of the U.S. population, religious upbringing is a strong predictor of adult religious belief and practice (Barry and Abo-Zena 2014, 9; Ecklund and Park 2009; Ecklund and Scheitle 2007; Gross and Simmons 2009). *The more religious people are, the more likely they are to have more children, and people are usually religious because they were raised that way.*

Despite some of the theoretical work I talked about in the paragraphs above, sociologists are not prophets. Or, at least not very good ones. The future can be predicted by any social science only within a (usually wide) margin of error, and only in terms of specific projections based on carefully measured trends. I can't say whether or not religion will go away in the future with any certainty, but I can say that based on trends that it didn't go away in the recent past as predicted, and it probably isn't going away any time soon. Furthermore, even if, in generations to come, religion does become largely irrelevant in the U.S. and the world over, it would still matter how religion *has shaped* the trends that connect the present to the past. Coming to terms with environmental change, or likely any other morally charged social phenomenon, means looking at the past and examining how things have (or haven't) changed since then. What matters, then, is that religion matters *now*, it mattered in the past, and it matters even if the future does bring long-predicted religious declines. In fact, in the U.S., looking at *disaffiliation*—how people raised religious are affected in terms of environmental attitudes after they leave religion later in life—is a central focus of this work (see chapter 3).

The *normative* aspect—that religion *ought to go away*—is a bit more difficult to address. Usually, this kind of argument is made using a list of what presumably religion "causes" or "doesn't cause." It would take me too far afield to try to address all of what religion does or doesn't cause, let alone stack up some kind of tally of whether its "bads" outweigh its "goods" (even if I thought I was qualified to do so—I am not). Sometimes the "badness" of religion is seen in terms of its linkage to conservative political beliefs—which it is, particularly in wealthier countries (Norris and Inglehart 2011, 196–214). Perhaps this definition of "badness" says more about the speaker than about religion itself. I am not convinced that religion is uniquely "good" or "bad," or even that it is necessarily that much more "conservative" than other kinds of institutions tend to be (see Szrot 2020a, b). Without belaboring the point further, and with a promise to visit religious *causality* or *motivations* in the next chapter, I offer a banal axiom of my own: religion, or something like it, is just something that people as social beings tend to do, to varying degrees. If religion does "go away" in the future, people will tend to gravitate toward other things that are "like" religion in some important sense.

Though secularization has not quite gone as advertised, since the mid-twentieth century, the U.S. religious landscape has changed in important ways. The biggest change has been a decline in Protestantism, and a matching rise among the religiously unaffiliated—the *nones*. There has also been an increase in the percentage of U.S.-Americans who are religious, but do not belong to Judeo-Christian faiths (Chaves 2017; Jones 2016). In other words, the U.S. has become more religiously unaffiliated and more multicultural, in terms of religious identity, and these trends have accelerated over the past three decades. Understanding how religious change is linked to U.S. responses to environmental change is a central issue. And, as noted before, *change* can take place across one or more of three different axes. First, there are the changes in religious belief and affiliation that take place within a person's lifetime. Second, religious responses to environmental change have taken place across generations. Third, levels of environmental concern may *fluctuate* up and down year by year based on changes in the social, political, and cultural landscape.

RELIGION AND ENVIRONMENTAL
CONCERN: A CRITICAL OVERVIEW

Religion is harder to measure than, say, age, political ideology, education, or region—factors so consistently related to concern about environmental change that they have been named "the Buttel model" after pioneering U.S. environmental sociologist Frederick H. Buttel (see Buttel 1979; Mohai and Twight 1987). This can make it difficult to get a clear picture of how religion predicts other attitudes, because results depend on how researchers decide to think about, measure, and study religion. It's not as though studying the religion–environment connection is something that can be easily done in a lab under controlled conditions, either. Neither religious beliefs nor environmental concern arose in a vacuum, separated from any confounding personal experiences or social factors. These pitfalls are no doubt familiar to fellow sociologists of religion, as well as social scientists more generally. But they also mean that figuring out what's really going on takes a lot of research over a long period of time. Despite these complications, much of the existing research on the religion–environment connection shows how and why religion should be taken seriously as part of the explanation for how people come to terms with environmental change. A lot of research has been conducted on "environmental concern" in the U.S., and how it may be predicted. A 2002 meta-analysis noted between 700 and 800 peer-reviewed published studies on environmental concern (see Dunlap and Jones 2002), but the work on the religion–environment connection in the U.S. is more modest, and findings are mixed (see Szrot 2019, 4–10). Different, and sometimes conflicting, results followed from different measures of religion and environmental concern, as well as from the year(s) in which studies were conducted. These mixed findings, and the explanations offered for them, bear upon the efforts to measure *change* that are at the heart of this book.

Most of the time, "strict" or "conservative" or "literal Bible believing" U.S.-American Protestants hold lower levels of environmental concern, on average (Eckberg and Blocker 1989; Guth et al. 1995; Hand and Van Liere 1984; Schwadel and Johnson 2017; Sherkat and Ellison 2007; Szrot 2019b). Stricter forms of Christianity resist what Charles Taylor calls "the immanent frame" (see Taylor 2007, 3), or a worldview which stresses the importance of human activity over divine intervention. Put simply, if a person's picture of the world focuses on divine power and salvation in the next world (rather than human action in this one), concern about the environment may seem secondary, a distraction, or even idolatrous. This possibility is examined in the coming pages. In studying religion and human social behavior, I often find that the relationship between theory and lived human experience is rarely so straightforward. Survey data also show that the devoutly religious are on average no less likely to identify as environmentalists than other groups (Kanagy and Nelsen 1993, 43), and there are Protestants of many backgrounds and worldviews who have actively addressed environmental issues in the past (Baugh 2017; Danielsen 2013; Ellingson 2016; Hayhoe and Farley 2011; Land and Moore 1992; Pogue 2016).

Some studies have found a moderate sort of environmentalism among a number of religious groups, or a *stewardship* orientation (see Eckberg and Blocker 1996; Kanagy and Nelsen 1995; Shaiko 1987). Others found that Christians remain less environmentally engaged than other religious groups and unaffiliated people in the U.S., but only in some ways (Clements et al. 2014; Sherkat and Ellison 2007; Truelove and Joireman 2009). Again, making sense of the religion–environment connection depends, to some extent, on how environmental concern is measured, as well as how religion is measured. More importantly than *how* may be *when:* hence, this story about coming to terms with environmental change through the lens of religion and the sacred *over time*. Personal religious views are diverse, and may change over a lifetime. *When* is environmental concern more likely to be linked to religious views across a lifetime? Also, religious views of environmental change are diverse, but how have religious *groups* responded differently to this change over time? Finally, how have other cultural, social, and political changes in the U.S. over the past several decades shaped these trends? In looking at these trends, I also had to make certain decisions in terms of how to measure both religion and environmental concern. I offer more detail on these in the next chapter. The data on which this story is based is not the final word, but a contribution to a bigger conversation that has unfolded, and is still unfolding. To address change over time, I also need ways to think about *how* and the *when* in order to separate what happens across individuals' lifetimes from what happens in the context of a person born into an institution such as a religious group. To do this, I draw on two popular concepts in sociology: *habitus* and *reflexivity*.

Religion, Environmental Concern, and Habitus

The word *habitus* was coined by influential cultural sociologist Pierre Bourdieu, and it basically means a "feel for the game" (Bourdieu 1993, 5). It is probably strange, and perhaps even a little offensive, to think of religion as a "game" people develop a "feel for." Bourdieu's work, like any good sociologist, has a way of making things that seem ordinary and comfortable look alien and unfamiliar—he applied this concept to people's artistic taste (Bourdieu 2002), as well as education (Bourdieu 1986). Thinking about religion as something *learned*, something that is a bit like getting a formal education or learning to appreciate art, means thinking about religion *culturally*—as part of a pattern of beliefs and behaviors into which persons are born, grow up, and live. Sociologist of religion Penny Edgell (2012) referred to approaches of this type as the *cultural sociology of religion.* And maybe this isn't so strange, after all, thinking of religion in these terms: religious beliefs and practices do not come from nowhere. People who are religious as adults were usually raised religious in religious families. Being religious, then, can be thought of as part of an identity established through childhood upbringing (Jenkins 1992). This *habitus* "imprints" on people in ways they themselves often take for granted, or do not even recognize, and this prepares them for life in a specific cultural setting (Shepherd 2010, 150–1; Webb et al. 2002). Neither parents and caregivers nor societies want children to grow into passive blobs of cultural ideas. They want children who take on those ideas as their own, to benefit from them and willingly transmit them as they grow and mature. "Successful transmission of religion requires youth to become agents of their own religion, not merely followers of their family's traditions" (Warner and Williams 2010, 163). If religious *habitus* shapes views of environmental change, then it starts in early childhood. And religious *habitus* continues shaping views of environmental change later in life, likely even among those who leave religion. This is put to the test in chapter 3.

People's views of environmental change can also be seen as a sort of *ecological habitus* (Ishihara 2018; Kasper 2009). Just as religious habitus is a "feel for the game" that begins in childhood but becomes second-nature over time, ecological habitus can be thought of as the kinds of *relationships* people learn to build with the natural world over a lifetime in their own cultural contexts. This includes whether, and to what extent, people think of the environment as a priority, in personal, political, or moral terms, as well as what kinds of behaviors in which they are, and are not, willing to engage. Rather than thinking of ecological habitus as something people either *have* or *don't have*, it is better thought of as something that develops differently in different cultural contexts. Similarly, people don't either have a religious habitus, or not; they have a *different* religious habitus depending on the context of their upbringing and adult connection to religious groups and practices. Both religion and environmental concern are, therefore, are related to one another culturally, and develop beginning at an early age. Not only does this aspect of culture begin early in life, but cultural attitudes are relatively *durable*, meaning they are fairly stable in individual people and groups, and tend to change across generations (see Vaisey and Lizardo 2016). A person born into a specific religious group may be different from someone born into the same group 20 or 30 years earlier, but people born in the same group, around the same time, are likely to be similar in certain ways. The ways in which they are similar are likely to follow them over the course of a lifetime.

Religion, Environmental Concern, and Reflexivity

That is only part of the story—culture and the personal level, which is the focus of chapter 3. At another level, the *institutional* level, which is the focus of chapters 4 and 5, things look rather different. Specifically, *how* and *why* are those two persons, born into the same religious group 20 or 30 years apart, different in terms of environmental concern? Asking this question means puncturing one of the most enduring myths of religion: that religious faith is resistant to change because it is, seemingly by definition, not self-critical or open to new information. As with other aspects of the secularization axiom, evidence is both mixed and contested (see Hamlin and Lodge 2006). On this basis, scholars sometimes suggest that there is something fundamentally different about *modern* and *traditional* ways of knowing and of being in the world, but I am not as sure a bright line can be drawn between them. Sometimes there is practical value in drawing such a line, perhaps to address different pressures placed on selves in a reflexive modernity, a runaway world, and a risk society (see Szrot 2019a). I will demonstrate in the coming chapters that religious groups, like the other kinds of institutions human beings inhabit, are self-reflective, or *reflexive*, responding to environmental change, and shaping levels of environmental concern.

It is true that some of the ways in which religion has changed in the U.S. reflect "resistance." For example, a growing *moral* tension between conservative Protestants and science has emerged over that time (Evans 2013). And as religion has become more tightly linked with conservative politics (Chaves 2017; Norris and Inglehart 2011, 206), lower levels of confidence in science among political conservatives have emerged (Gauchat 2012, see also Mooney 2005). This is only part of the story, however: over the past half-century, religious groups have also shifted, fragmented, and re-aligned, responding to both cultural shifts and internal pressures (see Hunter 1991; Jones 2016; Roof and McKinney 1992). Going back even further, environmental historians have argued that shared religious views underpinned the U.S. Progressive reform and Social Gospel movements of the late nineteenth and early twentieth century, including early conservation efforts (see Stoll 2006, 54). Religious groups in fact respond to social pressures in multiple ways: some withdraw from mainstream culture and society in order to preserve their cherished core values, others "dig in" and critically engage with moral, cultural, and political change, and still others embrace, internalize, or even spearhead social change. Religious institutions sometimes splinter amid such pressures, joining other institutions or creating new ones. The legacy of the cultural change in the U.S. is a testament to institutions' (both religious and secular) potential for dynamic shifts and stubborn resistance. As religion and ecology scholars John Grim and Mary Evelyn Tucker (2015) note, this is religion's potential to be both *limiting* and *liberating*.

Again, to be *reflexive* is to be self-reflective. Giddens (1990) offered a vision of *reflexivity* as "a defining characteristic of human action" (36) that matters even more now, as "social practices are constantly examined and reformed in the light of incoming information about those very practices" (38). This is what it means to be *reflexive*—to *reflect upon* the practices in which one is engaged, and the beliefs that underpin them. People are necessarily reflexive, as living beings are learning, assessing, and responding to a changing environment. Institutions are also reflexive, but differ from people in at least two important ways. Sociologist Christian Smith (2010) defines "social structures," (I use *institution* throughout this book instead for consistency and simplicity—may the social theorists forgive me) as "*actively sustained* by human behaviors, practices, and interactions" (322) and "not merely durable, but have specific *dynamic historical existences* involving generation, development, and change" (323). In short, *institutions last longer and change more slowly than persons, including in their responses to hazards*. If I am walking down a poorly lit street at night, and see a car driving erratically toward me, I can get out of the way. Institutions cannot respond as quickly to hazards—preserving the metaphor, the erratic driver would plow right into the side of the building in which the institution was housed (not that all institutions are necessarily *in buildings*). Figuring out how institutions respond to hazards means thinking about the human world at more than one level at the same time, and it also means thinking about things *over time*. Both are different facets or aspects of change.

CHAPTER SUMMARY: INTRODUCTION AND PLAN OF THE BOOK

To recap: environmental change is happening at an accelerating pace, such that people can increasingly witness it. The task is to come to terms with the change—*Die Verwandlung*. Because of the complexity of these problems, and how human decision-making is involved in constructing them, this cannot be done without drawing upon, and engaging with, diverse cultural and moral resources. For many, such resources may be found in religion. There are good reasons to challenge the idea that religion "is going away" in some permanent or inevitable way, as well as the idea that religious identity and tradition is fundamentally resistant to change or self-reflection. Religion is a source of durable cultural norms and values that develop early in life and may persist later in life even among those who leave the religion of their upbringing. It follows that religious engagement with environmental change means thinking differently about how people view the environment. In particular, religion is more likely to show up as long-term cultural and ethical change across generations. Secular approaches, on the other hand, tend to focus on "single-issue" political and economic policy reform, with priorities changing based on current need and focus (Smith and Pulver 2009, 156–9). Research on the religion–environment connection is mixed, partly because of the differences in what is measured, as well as *when* it was measured. Pulling together these several threads, I restate that understanding how religious groups, traditions, and institutions respond to environmental change requires assessing *change over time*.

Assessing change over time is a tricky business. When and where there is enough data to do it, there is, first of all, the problem of *dependency* (see Hoffman 2015, 17–9). It is a problem I have hinted at more than once already, but feel I should more carefully explain before moving forward. If my childhood friend and I were to compare our grades from first until sixth grade, there are three ways in which we might be statistically different. The first possibility is that my friend's grades might be better than mine on average because she is a higher achiever overall. She just tends to consistently earn better grades, and seemingly always has. The second is that I might slowly "catch up to" or "fall further behind" my childhood friend over time, because our grades change at different rates. Maybe I started off ahead in first grade, but started slacking off and fell behind by sixth. Finally, our grades might be closer together, or farther apart, because of *when* they were assessed in time, for reasons that are not related to differences in our individual ability levels. Maybe my dog really did start eating my math homework in the fourth grade.

Something similar happens when it comes to measuring environmental concern, or anything else, over time. The earliest studies on environmental concern consistently showed that age is *negatively* related to environmental concern, meaning older people, on average, are less likely to express environmental concern (Buttel 1979). There are actually three reasons why this could be the case. First, it is possible that people in fact tend to care less about the environment as they get older. Maybe they have other priorities later in life, are concerned about the economic consequences that will befall them from aggressive environmental legislation, or assume the riskiest of the environmental changes will not happen until long after they are gone. This is a genuine *age effect*: it's driven by the way individual people actually change over individual lifetimes.

It's also possible that older people are less environmentally concerned because environmental concern is a more durable attitude across people's lifetimes. That is, the way people understand the connection between humans and nature is learned and internalized earlier in life. This means that environmental concern does not decrease with age. Instead, it *increases* based on when a person was born. This second kind of effect is called a *cohort effect*. Environmental concern, especially through the lens of religion, is expected to grow slowly across generations of people, rather than declining as individual people get older. With a cohort effect, it's not that people care less about the environment as they get older. It's that millennials care more than baby boomers about the environment on average.

Finally, if the data are actually collected over a period of time rather than at a single time point, then maybe environmental concern depends less on how old people are or when they are born than it does on the things that are happening around them in the year they are surveyed. If massive environmental changes are part of the news cycle, political debates, or people's experiences one year, then they may respond to these cues by expressing more, or less, environmental concern. This is what is called a *period effect*. As will become clear, these are usually not "either–or" but happen to different degrees all at once.

That's the *how*; now, for the *why*. The concepts of *reflexivity* and *habitus* are differences of *emphasis*. They are two different ways to think about people and groups over time that are in tension with one another. People are born into, and learn, certain ideas about the relationship between human beings, nature, and the sacred in the form of a *habitus*. This habitus is something people begin to internalize, culturally, from a very early age. If religious habitus and ecological habitus are connected, then people should show meaningful differences in environmental concern based on the religion in which they are raised. The easiest way to tell if this is true is to compare religious people who remain within the religion in which they are raised to religious people who *disaffiliate*, or leave the religion of their upbringing and do not embrace another religion. Studying habitus also suggests that measuring the effects of religion should focus on changes across generations, or birth cohorts (cohort effects rather than age effects).

Yes, people can be reflexive, too. However, the focus on culture and morality means it is religious *groups* that are expected to be reflexive over time as they come to terms with environmental change. This, again, means focusing on cohort effects, especially how people in religious groups change across generations. Research has shown that culture is relatively durable over people's lifetimes when it comes to values and morality (see Vaisey and Lizardo 2016), a reason why this work focuses a lot on birth cohorts or generations (may the life course scholars forgive me for conflating the two!).

To be clear, I am not in the habit of assuming what I am trying to find out. Hundreds of models based on different assumptions were estimated before the first word of this book was ever written. These models are best thought of as the major events within the story, but are not the story itself. The gritty details of model-centered research belong to expert journals. In many cases I cite such work, and take the time to explain the methods and models, but I keep the methods talk to a minimum, use percentages when referencing these models, and focus on explaining what I've found and what it means rather than exhaustively describing every result. Focusing on telling the story, I hope to shed additional light on how religion explains environmental concern, as well as how religion might play a role in addressing environmental change in the future.

There are five more chapters to come. In chapter 2, I aim to (1) take religion seriously as motivating other attitudes and behaviors, including environmental concern; (2) describe how religion, environmental concern, and other factors were measured; and (3) explain the math and model-building without resorting to (much) statistical jargon. Chapter 3 focuses on the role of religious *upbringing* in predicting environmental concern, as well as the role of adult *disaffiliation*, or leaving religion. Explanations for disaffiliation are briefly examined, as are differences in levels of environmental concern among different groups within the ranks of the religiously unaffiliated. The role of habitus in particular is re-examined here, as well. Chapters 4 and 5 complicate and challenge what happens in chapter 3. Chapter 4 expands on the story in chapter 3 by first focusing on birth cohorts: the "big picture." Some smaller, non-Judeo-Christian religious groups are discussed briefly, as are explanations for reflexivity in environmental change across religious groups. In this spirit, chapter 4 also separates out and examines *age* and *period* effects using a series of more complex models. Chapter 5 brings in insights related to race, class, gender, and partisan political differences in levels of environmental concern. Comparing women to men, low- and high-income U.S.-Americans to the middle classes, Republicans to Democrats, and Blacks to whites complicates matters, but also shows how and why religion, in terms of both habitus and reflexivity, matters as an explanation. Finally, chapter 6 draws together and revisits the findings and insights from the previous chapters, offering broader visions of addressing risk as well as some ways forward, in terms of future study and practical engagement.

Chapter 2

Religion and Change over Time

Half a millennium ago, the promise of conquest and riches brought European explorer-warriors—*conquistadores*—to American shores. These interlopers often viewed the Indigenous peoples they met as subhuman, to be captured and sold into slavery if not killed outright. On the heels of tales of butchery, Pope Paul III issued the 1537 Encyclical letter *Pastorale Officium* (Encyclical letters are issued by popes, and become official Catholic doctrine) which "proclaimed the dignity and rights of the native peoples of the Americas by insisting that they not be deprived of their freedom or the possession of their property" (quoted in John Paul II 1987, 3). Catholics flocking to the "New World" henceforth were expected to treat the native peoples with dignity and respect. However, Catholic in name, *conquistadores* often ignored the Church's mandate when it stood in the way of plunder (Fisher 2000, 15).

One year before the 2016 race for the U.S. presidency, Pope Francis (2015) issued *Laudato si'*, an Encyclical letter that has come to be called "the climate change Encyclical" due to its sweeping emphasis on environmental change broadly, and the hazards of climate change specifically. It may be one of the most widely discussed events in the history of religion and ecology to date (see Brulle and Antonio 2015; Carvalho 2015; Edenhofer et al. 2015; Ehrlich and Harte 2015; Jenkins 2018; Raven 2016; Szrot 2020a; Tucker and Grim 2016; Wright 2015). At the same time, bystanders noted the state of U.S. environmental politics: "As one despairing, Republican-voting meteorologist put it, climate science [denial] has become 'a bizarre litmus test for conservatism'" (Hamilton 2013, 88). Republican presidential contender Jeb Bush, identifying as a practicing Catholic, responded to the Encyclical on the campaign trail thusly: "'I hope I'm not going to get castigated for saying this by my priest back home. But I don't get economic policy from my bishops or my cardinals or my pope,'...religion 'ought to be about making us better

as people, less about things [that] end up getting into the political realm'"
(quoted in Hale 2015).

To be clear, I am not comparing presidential hopefuls to *conquistadores*.
Instead, these tales reveal difficulties in offering religion as an explanation
for attitudes or behaviors. At the risk of stating the obvious, religious people
sometimes ignore or defy the rules of their own religious beliefs, especially
when the stakes are high enough. This leads to charges of hypocrisy, but often
critics of religion go further, seizing on these examples to argue something
which includes the phrase: *this person in this place at this time is not following the rules of their own religion because religion is nothing but . . .* Physicist
Paul Davies (1983) has referred to this as "nothing but-tery," a peculiar form
of *reductionism* (58–71). In this case, it is an attempt to reduce religion in its
entirety to some decidedly nonreligious something else. This raises an important question: how does religion actually influence other attitudes and behaviors, and how can those who study it know that it's *really* religion, and not some
decidedly nonreligious something else, that is doing the influencing?

I am not arguing that religion is more important than other explanatory
factors, such as politics or economics, nor that it is completely free of their
influence. Instead, I am asking *what it would mean* for religion to predict
environmental concern in ways that cannot be explained away as "nothing
but" something else. This chapter does three things. First, I visit different
kinds of religious *motives*. Second, I address the *variables* in question—that
is, how is religion measured, and how do I make sure that religion, and
not something else, is actually doing the explaining? Finally, I explain the
methods used to compare the variables. This chapter does not deal directly
with research findings, or explanations for them, but instead is devoted to the
methodology that defines the project—a systematic but accessible study of
the methods used, and an explanation for how and why these methods were
chosen over others.

(NOT) PRACTICING WHAT WE PREACH

Catholic *conquistadores* ignored papal decree; a Catholic presidential hope-
ful hedged on the climate change Encyclical. This is not unusual: what
sociologist Mark Chaves called *religious incongruence* is widespread and
pervasive (Chaves 2010). It probably isn't that surprising that people often
don't "practice what they preach." Not only do sociologists often expect it,
but it is in my view one of the most interesting things about the job. To show
that religious incongruence is both real and widespread, Chaves (2010) noted
an ordained Church of Christ minister who lost faith in God (1), believers in
faith healing who *also* seek scientific medical care, and athletes who believe

superstitions improve their play but still train hard (3). He also reported that, according to survey data, conservative Protestants watch X-rated movies, and have sex outside marriage, at rates similar to other groups (5).

If the evidence does not match the assumptions, then there is something wrong with the assumptions. *Why don't people consistently and automatically follow the dictates of their religion?* is probably the wrong question to ask. A better question is: *Why assume that the link between religious beliefs and other attitudes or behaviors is straightforward?* With Chaves, I reject the package of assumptions he calls the *religious congruence fallacy*, noting that this fallacy lies behind many secular criticisms of religion, as well as the demonization of other, particularly Islamic, religions and civilizations (Chaves 2010). For me, doing away with the flawed assumption of religious congruence makes space for more careful thinking about religion in terms of culture. This includes *habitus*—what kinds of "second-nature" beliefs and behaviors connect religion to environmental concern—as well as *reflexive* institutions which change over time, shaping (and shaped by) their members in the process. Religion, like all things involving human beings, is full of ambiguity and flux. In fact, religious incongruity may have increased in the U.S. over the past half-century. Sociologists Wade Clark Roof and William McKinney referred to this as "the new voluntarism," a strongly democratic, individualistic view of religion in the U.S., in which the religious authority often takes a back seat to personal choice and voluntary commitment (Roof and McKinney 1992, 40–71). In other words, people emphasize, or de-emphasize, aspects of their faith based on other, competing ideals, commitments, and identities. This does not mean religion is irrelevant—far from it. It simply means that religious beliefs don't exist in a social vacuum.

There are two ways to address this ambiguity, flux, and religious incongruity. First, I need a way to capture and compare the complexity of religious motivations. Fortunately, I can draw on what others have already done, to create a typology of religious motives which fits the scope of this particular story. Second, I take for granted that religion is one of many factors that influence environmental concern. That means comparing the effects of many factors at the same time, figure out whether it is in fact religion and not something else doing the explaining. This involves detailing how religion is measured throughout the rest of this work, as well as some of the other *controls* used to capture other aspects of a person's life, identity, values, or culture that may also influence environmental concern.

Comparing Religious Motivations

There are many avenues of potential religious influence. Sociologist of religion Mark Regnerus' (2006) work *Forbidden Fruit*, which addresses

religion and sexuality among adolescents and emerging adults, offers some
guidance in the form of a typology (184–5). Environmental concern is obvi-
ously not adolescent sexuality. However, the connection between religion and
environmental change includes some overlapping kinds of ambivalence and
incongruity. After briefly describing the six types of religious motives from
Regnerus' work, I build on three types of motives to create a typology of my
own that is appropriate to the project at hand.

The first type is *intentional action:* people know that religion is impacting
their decision-making. This means religious people are able to show why
they are environmentally concerned, and that *why* can be stated in religious
terms. In the current context, that would mean: *I am religious, and I care
about the environment, because these specific aspects of my religion tell me
that I must do so.* The second is *instrumental religion:* in this case, the reasoning process links to religion in some way, but the reasoning is coming from
some other source. In this case, people may be environmentally concerned
because they are directly affected by environmental change, and may "bring
in religion" for practical or strategic reasons. *I am religious, and I care about
the environment, but I don't care about the environment directly because my
religion tells me I must do so. Instead, I have found ways to "build a bridge"
between what I take to be my religious worldview and my reasons for caring
about the environment, which were not originally part of my religion.* The
third type is *invisible religion:* religion influences persons' actions, but they
may themselves be unaware of it, or even deny that religion is the source of
influence. This is the kind of thing that is hard to detect by directly asking
people, but the kind of thing that can be found using survey data. If a lot of
people in a religious group are also concerned about the environment, but it
doesn't seem to be directly connected to the religious beliefs *per se*, then it is
something that people in that religion tend to be exposed to more often. For
example: *I was raised in this religious tradition, and people in this religious
tradition tended to be a part of youth groups, activities, and organizations
which generated appreciation for nature from an early age. It isn't religion,
but the connection religion has to other institutions, that leads to higher levels of environmental concern. I am likely not directly aware of how religion
has had this effect on my life.* I am particularly interested in some version of
these three motives.

I'll briefly note the other three types for comparison, but they are not part
of the analysis. A fourth type is *inconsistent religion,* involving a situation
in which a person believes religion should be influential, but it is not. In this
case, people who are a member of a certain religion know they're *supposed
to* care about the environment, but they, by and large, don't. *I know that
my faith tells me that the environment is important, but I just cannot bring
myself to follow through with the things I need to do in order to make the*

connection at a personal level. This would be interesting to learn, but big-picture data analysis and storytelling don't provide the information needed to compare words and deeds in this way. Similarly, with the fifth type, *irrelevant religion,* which involves the belief that religion is not influential, and should not be. *Religion has nothing to do with my beliefs about the environment, nor should it.* It is hard to say, with a "big-picture" analysis like this one, whether or not people *want* religion to influence their environmental attitudes. Finally, *irreligion* means religion has no influence. *I am not religious, so religion does not influence me in environmental matters, or much else.* Directly, a person could claim that religion has no influence, or that it does not apply, but this does not necessarily mean that religion *in fact* has no influence. It is possible that someone who has shed the religion of their upbringing still bears the stamp of its *influence.* This can be tested, at least indirectly, by comparing the effects of religious *upbringing* and *disaffiliation* (chapter 3).

Without interviews or some other method, it's not possible to detect what people think they *should be* doing (which rules out inconsistent, irrelevant, and irreligious motivations). I can, however, explain what I find by building on this typology of motives a bit. For instance, if there's a clear and intentional link between religion and environmental concern, then this link should be stronger for those who are "closer to" their religion. People who go to religious services more often, or hold their faith in higher esteem, should have levels of environmental concern that reflect this direct commitment. If religion plays an *instrumental* role in environmental concern, people who are already more likely to express environmental concern—younger, politically liberal, urban-dwelling, and more highly educated, per the Buttel model (1979)—will express more environmental concern. *Invisible religion,* or religious influence people are unaware of, may be the most interesting possibility in this story. A link between religion and environmental concern is possible, even if those who are religious typically do not know why such a link exists. Religious groups may become "greener" over time in terms of doctrine and practice in ways that the average member of the group isn't even aware of. Religious organizations may also raise people into greener beliefs, habits, and lifestyles by connecting people to other "greener" organizations, groups, and practices in ways that go largely unnoticed by believers in the context of their faith. This would be a matter of habitus, existing "second-nature" to those who have it even though they aren't really aware of how religion resulted in such beliefs. Also, people may leave the religion of their childhood upbringing and retain aspects of that way of life into adulthood, which may include higher levels of environmental concern.

To recap, this means there are three types of religious motivation that I'll be focusing on here, referred to as follows. Type 1 is *direct motive:* religion *is the* reason why people are more, or less, environmentally concerned. If this is the case, then (1) people who are *more religious* within a religious group should be *more environmentally concerned* (and vice versa), and (2) people raised in religious groups that have official pro-environmental doctrine or statements should have higher levels of environmental concern. Type 2 is *indirect motive:* religion and environment are connected for people "after the fact" through a reasoning process that is not directly religious. If this is the case, then (1) people who would otherwise be more likely to be environmentally concerned anyway based on past research will also be more likely to be environmentally concerned, and (2) differences between religious groups won't matter that much when these other factors are added into the mix. Type 3 is *invisible motive:* it is not clear that people are even aware of the religious influence on their environmental views. If this is the case, then (1) people raised in a religion with historically higher levels of environmental concern will be more environmentally concerned, and (2) those effects will remain even among those who leave that religion later in life.

Religion as Habitus

Now, armed with a way to make sense of how religion influences people, I return to *habitus* and *reflexivity.* I'll start with *habitus,* as it's the first thing that I'll look at, and it's also probably the simplest to describe. Recall in the last chapter the definition of *habitus* as a "feel for the game" (Bourdieu 1993, 5); in his groundbreaking work *Distinction: A Social Critique of the Judgement of Taste,* sociologist Pierre Bourdieu defined *habitus* in greater detail:

> The habitus is necessity internalized and converted into a disposition that generates meaningful practices and meaning-giving perceptions; it is a general, transposable disposition that carries out a systematic, universal application—beyond the limits of what has been directly learnt—of the necessity inherent in the learning conditions. That is why an agent's whole set of practices are both systematic, inasmuch as they are the product of the application of identical schemes, and systematically distinct from the practices constituting another life-style (Bourdieu 2002, 170).

In trying to make sense of how background cultural factors influence a person's education, Bourdieu noted further that, "cultural capital can be acquired, to a varying extent, depending on the period, the society, and the social class, in the absence of any deliberate inculcation, and therefore quite unconscious" (Bourdieu 1986, 48–9). Bourdieu was originally trying to understand social inequality in novel ways. People learn how to *be,* within a certain cultural context, from the moment of birth. Each person is assigned a sex, and has a family or caregiver(s) who take responsibility for development early in life. There are differences in how people are raised based on who that family is, what they do in their free time, what they eat or wear, and how they speak. All of these are things that people make part of themselves over time, often in ways they themselves do not even realize.

Religion can be thought of as a practice, and a set of "internal dispositions," as well. Having been raised Roman Catholic, I learned many beliefs and practices that shaped (and continue to shape) the way I view, and live in, the world. Going to Mass involved learning when to stand, sit, and kneel, how and when to pray, what words to say, what songs to sing, how to receive communion, confess sins, and why each of these acts was religiously significant, among other things. As a child I learned a Catholic *habitus,* or a bundle of practices that identified and distinguished me as a Catholic. Many of those practices are *durable;* they do not simply leave me, but are part of me, and still influence me, even if and when I am not aware of it. My parents played a notable role in this process; they decided to raise me in this way. As a person raised Catholic, and through attending religious services as well as other events hosted by the faith-based community of which I was a part, I interacted with other children, and my parents, with other adults, in a broader social network. Somewhere in this bundle of practices, internal dispositions, and connections to social networks, I became interested in the relationship between nature and the sacred, which in turn led to a research topic, a career choice, a book.

Religious motives begin early in life, because religious influence is a durable element of who we are, and who we become. In this way, it's possible to make sense of religious motivations, whether direct, indirect, or invisible (Types 1, 2, and 3, respectively). Understanding religion as a habitus that can contribute, directly or indirectly, to environmental concern helps to establish a connection. Furthermore, understanding *habitus* as something that is partly unconscious or "second-nature" allows me to sidestep some theoretical difficulties related to comparing religious groups. For example, how do Methodists know how they're different from Baptists? If religion can be thought of as a habitus, then people cannot be expected to know all the ways in which their religion differs from others. Most people, most of the time, are not even fully conscious of the many ways in which their own religion has *made them different.*

This may sound like destiny, but I do not mean to be so fatalistic. Commentators have noted the "conservative" nature of *habitus* in a variety of contexts—as something that people "grow into" that is often part of them without their direct knowledge, it can be quite resistant to change (see Kirby 2020, 91). Sociology is also the study of networks, institutions, and structures—the kinds of things that people build, sustain, and participate in. I noted some properties of structures which could be applied to organizations or institutions in chapter 1; they must "make order out of some set of things [, and] they do this work because they endure for a time" (Lemert 2012, 123–6). The lives of humans, as social animals, are structured by a vast number of influences. That doesn't mean people are "blank slates" waiting for society to impose its will (see Pinker 2016; Schut et al. 2020); human beings are dynamic living creatures who react to, and interact with, the environment and the people in it. People have an inborn capacity to be *reflexive,* or self-reflective, a capacity that also exists in institutions.

Reflexivity as "Living Tradition"

In fact, it is this capacity for change, and the human ability to come to terms with change, that animates this work. Without *reflexivity,* the problems related to religious (in)congruity would never arise: people raised in a faith would fully internalize all of its rules, norms, and strictures, and would act on them in predictable and orderly ways. Fortunately, human beings do not work this way—sociology would probably be easier to do, but life would be incredibly dull.

Reflexivity also operates at the "bigger" institutional, structural, and society-wide levels, as noted in the previous chapter. Rather than a fixed set of doctrines, religious institutions (like other kinds of institutions) change over time, responding to the internal pressures of memberships and external pressures of the cultural environment. For example, in *The Historical Roots of Our Ecological Crisis,* historian Lynn White, Jr. argued provocatively that, "especially in its Western form, Christianity is the most anthropocentric religion the world has seen" (White 1967, 1205). This is sometimes offered, and tested, as an explanation for religious *anthropocentrism*—a human-centered rather than "nature-centered" worldview—among Christians (see, for example, Djupe and Hunt 2009; Eckberg and Blocker 1989; Szrot 2019b; Whitney 1993). What is less commonly noted is that, although White was making a historical, descriptive argument, his goal as both a scholar and an environmentally concerned Christian was to seek "greener" representatives for a "greener" Christianity (see Nash 1996, 194–204). In the present context, White's work offered both external (as an environmentalist and environmental historian) and internal (as a Christian) pressures for greater *reflexivity* among Christians regarding environmental concern.

Of course, not every religious group responds to such pressures in the same ways. Though some might embrace the criticism as constructive, and act accordingly, others might reject such criticism, or even become *less* environmentally concerned if perceiving this line of thought as an attack on their way of life. White himself offered Saint Francis of Assisi as an avatar of a greener Christianity; Francis has been widely heralded since as an exemplar of the compatibility of Christianity with greater environmental concern (White 1967, 1206–7). For example, the current Catholic pope, Francis, bears his namesake, and the connection is explicit: in 1979, the Catholic Church declared Saint Francis the patron saint of ecology (John Paul II 1979). Additionally, the Catholic Church, through the official pronouncements of popes since the mid-twentieth century, has become increasingly "green" in its doctrine, incorporating environmental concern into social teaching (see Szrot 2020a).

Catholicism is hardly the only example of *reflexivity* regarding environmental change in the U.S., nor should the world's more than one billion Catholics be viewed as a "unified front" on environmental issues (or much else, for that matter). In line with religious incongruence, just because church doctrine tells people to do something doesn't mean they actually do it. But it is interesting that studies of church doctrine place the first official stirrings of contemporary religious environmental concern among Protestant denominations as early as 1971, beginning with the United Presbyterian Church, with many denominations, religious groups, and prominent religious leaders following (Gottlieb 1996, 194–316; Shaiko 1987; Yaple 1982). Southern Baptists have published literature on sacred duties to the environment (Land and Moore 1992), and some of the U.S.'s more theologically conservative Protestants have spoken out on environmental concern, though their efforts have met with mixed reactions among religious leaders (Danielsen 2013; Ellingson 2016, 55), perhaps due to growing political and cultural polarization (Hunter 1991; Pogue 2016). Indirectly, environmentalism itself has been called a "quasi-religious movement" rooted in strands of Reformed Protestantism that can be traced back to the New England Puritans, and carried through to the twentieth century by Presbyterians and other "mainline Protestant" organizations (see Stoll 2015). In short, Baptists, Methodists, Presbyterians, Lutherans, and Episcopalians, as well as Catholics, have a history of environmental commitments and engagements. Some of these dated back a century or more, but most of these commitments became more clearly articulated in the last three decades of the twentieth century.

Zooming out, this means that any date I choose for "the first stirrings of environmental engagement among religious groups" is going to involve "starting in the middle" and risking leaving out important parts of the past. The mid-twentieth century was also a time of historic cultural change. In particular, modern secular environmentalism took off with Rachel Carson's *Silent Spring*—a work detailing the potentially widespread, long-term dangers of pesticides (Carson 1962). On the other hand, "wilderness" as a soteriological (or salvation-rooted) vision emerged much earlier, arising in the nineteenth century and coming of age in the early twentieth century (Berry 2015, 120–46). Going back further, there is evidence of an ecologically moderate "stewardship" ethic among the Puritans, which was later adopted by Presbyterians, and seems to have profoundly shaped the U.S.-American Progressive movement toward environmental conservation (see Purdy 2015; Stoll 2015). The First Peoples and cultures of the world could likely trace their views of nature and the proper human place in it over millennia. Explaining trends means taking seriously these historical developments, but it also means being attentive to when trend lines change, and what historical developments are close to those changes. Far from a uniformly staid or reactionary view of environmental change, religious groups in the U.S. have undergone numerous changes in environmental views and engagements, some of which have deep historical roots. Two broad and fairly historically stable dimensions of this change—*conservation* and *stewardship*—emerge from briefly visiting these changes.

MEASURING SOCIAL TRENDS

Given that *change* in religious groups' attitudes toward environmental issues is not only expected, but lines up with historical evidence, how can I best capture and describe this change in terms of sociological *trends*? Answering that question means speaking the language of data and variables, measurement and method. Put simply, I'm looking at how religion *predicts* environmental concern (the *outcome*), alongside other aspects of life that might also predict environmental concern (*controls*). The rest of this chapter explains where the data came from, how they have been used to capture religion, environmental concern, and change over time, and a brief description of the mathematical models that are highlighted in the next three chapters. As someone who is passionate about statistics and research methods (my wife makes fun of me for admitting that), I hope this section will be accessible and helpful, and that I did not "overdo" it.

Measuring change means having access to data collected over a period of time. This work is based on the results of a project which used publicly available data downloaded from the General Social Survey, a large-scale, nationally representative survey conducted every year between 1972 and 1994 (except for 1979, 1981, and 1992) and every other year beginning in 1996 (Smith et al. 2015). With guidance and support from scholars in sociology, quantitative research methods, environmental studies, and physics, I developed and carried out the research on which this book is based between the summer of 2016 and the spring of 2019, and more technical details can be found in the original report (see Szrot 2019). I am not the first person to study environmental concern using this data, but relatively few other studies have dealt specifically with religion, and only three published studies to my knowledge have captured change in environmental concern as a function of religion, all of which were conducted while this work was in progress (Carlisle and Clark 2018; Konisky 2018; Schwadel and Johnson 2017).

Religious Groups and Religious Motives

There are a few popular ways to measure religion among sociologists. One approach, called FUND, captures theological differences between U.S.-American religious groups, particularly Protestants (see Smith 1990). *Fundamentalists,* in this scheme, stress the literal and inerrant truth of Scripture (including the End Times prophecies) and the importance of a personal "born-again" experience, whereas *liberals* support modernization, science, and activity in this world, opposing literal readings of the Bible (Smith 1990, 226). *Moderates* fall somewhere in between. I use these distinctions to make broad comparisons. They were also used to measure change over time by year and age (see chapter 4), and to separate groups of *other Protestants*. Another approach, RELTRAD, was developed to capture differences between religious groups, especially U.S. Protestants. In this one, evangelical (conservative) and mainline (moderate/liberal) Protestants are separated out, as are black Protestants, and compared to Roman Catholics, Jewish persons, other religion, and the unaffiliated (see Steensland et al. 2000). I refer to the distinctiveness of evangelical and mainline Protestant groups at times, as well as the differences between black and white Protestants within the same denomination. Finally, the General Social Survey variable *feelings about the Bible* (whether literal word of God, inspired word, a book of fables written by men) is used for those who aim to compare groups of U.S. Christians specifically. I use this to test for "closeness to religion" in some models.

Every research effort in the social sciences involves a long series of decisions. These decisions are guided by the question one is trying to answer, as well as the existing theory/research (in that order). In this case, to know whether, and to what extent, religion (1) shapes individual *habitus,* as well as (2) the extent to which religious groups have shown *reflexivity* regarding environmental change, I had to more narrowly define the religious groups that are doing the shaping and the self-reflecting. I divided religious identity into several categories that are recognizable and have some degree of historical continuity (even if there have been internal shifts and divisions, particularly in recent decades). To speak the language of research methods, I did this by merging three variables: *religious affiliation, religious denomination,* and *fundamentalism.* This resulted in 13 distinct *religious groups* with relatively historically stable meanings: *Baptist, Methodist, Lutheran, Presbyterian, Nondenominational, fundamentalist other Protestant, moderate other Protestant, liberal other Protestant, Catholic, Jewish, other religion, and none.* In assuming that religion is something most people are usually "born into," I used religious *upbringing* rather than religious *identity* to start things off in chapter 3. This allowed me to compare people who remained in the religion of their upbringing to those who left that faith to become *unaffiliated* and look for evidence of Type 3, or invisible, motives.

Because religious identity is only one of many facets of a person's religion, and because I am interested in finding out more specifically how religion *motivates* environmental concern, I also added some additional religion measures. Recall that there are three types of religious motivations that will be examined in this book. Type 1, or *direct motive,* Type 2, or *indirect motive,* and Type 3, or *invisible motive.* If religion is directly motivating environmental concern (Type 1), then the "closer to" a person's religion they are on average, the more environmentally concerned they should be. If religion motivates environmental concern indirectly (Type 2), then people who are already more likely to be environmentally concerned on average are going to be more environmentally concerned regardless of religious identity. And if religion motivates environmental concern in ways that people aren't themselves even aware of (Type 3), then people raised in religions with a history of environmental concern will be more environmentally concerned whether or not they remain religious in adulthood. Closeness to religion, then, is largely a way to test for Type 1 motives. I used three measures of closeness to religion: whether or not one attends religious services at least once a week, whether or not one has high levels of confidence in organized religion, and *feelings about the Bible* (though it is also only available after 1984) to establish whether it was the religious group itself or some aspect of theology that better predicted environmental concern. There are some additional variations in terms of measuring and comparing religion, but I'll hold off on describing those until the next chapters.

Generations versus Birth Cohorts

In chapter 4, the focus shifts from individual changes involving upbringing and disaffiliation to intergenerational change over long periods of time. The language of "generations" is a major part of popular conversations about cultural change. The sniping between "boomers" and "millennials" is a reflection of how culturally divided the U.S. is, and how those cultural divides are rooted in a disconnect between a not-so-distant past and a rapidly changing present. But "generation" is a far from straightforward concept. Cut-off points for generations can seem arbitrary, and are different depending on who is making the decisions: is a person born in 1980 really that different on average from a person born in 1979? Sociologist Karl Mannheim (1952) added another layer of complexity to this by arguing that shared generational experiences must be part of a "generations" story, meaning that people technically belong to multiple generations *at the same time*. In other words, deciding who is in what generation requires some thought, and there is no perfect way to do so.

To sidestep some of these difficulties, I created *birth cohorts*. Put simply, birth cohorts are collections of years (in this case, roughly 15-year intervals) into which people are born. They are the simplest way to measure change over time, and using them fits with the theory developed in this book so far (that culture is relatively durable) and some of the questions that arose out of it. To create cohorts, I just subtracted *age* from *year* to calculate *birth years*. Because year ranged from 1973 to 2014, and the age ranged from 18 to 89 (89 was entered for those 89 or older), birth years ranged from 1884 (someone 89 years old, surveyed in 1973) to 1996 (someone 18 years old, surveyed in 2014). These were then arranged into seven cohorts. It may help to think of cohort 4 as *boomers* (born between 1950 and 1964), cohort 5 as *generation X* (1965–1979), and cohort 6 as *millennials* (1980 or later), roughly speaking. Though results in chapters 4 and 5 are framed in terms of these numbered cohorts (0–6), I will at times alternate between talking about generations and talking about cohorts to keep it simple.

Again, there are three ways that things can change over time. In addition to figuring out whether, and to what extent, religious persons changed with upbringing and disaffiliation (chapter 3), and how religious groups changed over time regarding environmental concern (chapter 4), I had to be mindful of these three ways things can change. It is possible change can be explained in terms of *cohort* effects, or changes rooted in when people were born, *age* effects, or changes over the course of a person's lifetime, or *period* effects, or changes in environmental concern, year by year, across the U.S. as a whole. If, and to what extent, there really has been *cultural* change in environmental concern, then changes would occur across birth cohorts. If, on the other hand, people change with age, or by year, this would suggest that explanations are more "secular"—political and economic changes within the U.S. as a whole, or changes in personal political and economic attitudes on average. That means ruling out age and year (chapter 4), as well as other possible effects (chapter 5).

This is probably as good a place as any to point out that model-building is always an imperfect endeavor—models can even be thought of as "simplifications" or "useful stories" based on a partial understanding of the social world and built according to certain assumptions. This is one reason why I have built so many different kinds of models, to see if they agree with one another, and how they line up with other research based on different assumptions. It is also true that model-building can at best allow us to be "less wrong" about certain things, but due to the complexity of the social world and the vastness of the variables that shape human lives and societies, sociology doesn't produce universal laws that can be expressed mathematically the way that physics does (though there are some who would debate with me on that). Again, this makes sociology harder to do, but keeps life far more interesting. I like to remind my friends, my students, and myself, that on the best of days, social scientists can predict maybe 25% of what happened, or what's going to happen (and often less). It is necessary to *interpret* this information in the context of what others have found, "connecting the dots" to develop a theory or general explanation for what's happening and why.

Environmental Concern and Other Important Variables

If religion and changes over time (by cohort, age, and year) *predict* environmental concern (as is the assumption of this work), then religion, change over time, and the rest of the control variables are the *predictors,* and environmental concern is the *outcome.* Measuring environmental concern is the simplest to explain, but simplicity means limitations. Two environmental concern outcomes are used. As with some of the measures of closeness to religion, they may be thought of as approximations for environmental concern, and have been treated as such. *Stewardship* involves doing more to improve and protect the environment, and *conservation* means doing more for national parks and recreation.

Figuring out whether it is "really" religion and not something else means *controlling for* other possible predictors of environmental concern, as they relate to existing studies on the subject. This also allows me to distinguish between Type 1 (direct) and Type 2 (indirect) motive in terms of environmental concern. If groups that are already to more likely to be environmentally concerned remain so when adding religion, then this suggests a Type 2 motive at work. The first set of control variables involves *attitudes.* I have already mentioned religious closeness—whether or not people go to church at least once a week, have high confidence in organized religion, and how they feel about the Bible. Another important variable for measuring attitudes is *high trust in the scientific community.* This is a way to approximate what Charles Taylor (2007) called "the immanent frame"—a worldview which stresses "this-worldly" human activity over divine intervention (3). That is, to what extent do things in the world change because human beings take action to change them, and to what extent does change come from a God or higher power? It is probably too simplistic to argue that science and religion are at odds with one another (see, for example, Ecklund et al. 2019; Evans 2013; Gross and Simmons 2009; Scheitle 2011), but some religious worldviews are more, or less, in tension with scientific knowledge and processes which reside in the "immanent frame." For example, perhaps more *fundamentalist* religious groups are less concerned about the environment, because a theology that stresses the role of the divine over human activity may simply not align with such concerns.

Another measure of attitudes that has had a clear impact on environmental concern in ongoing debates was political party identity. I have grouped together Republican/lean Republican and Democrat/lean Democrat, and compared them to people who are Independents, members of other political parties, or otherwise identify as neither. In chapter 5, I use these distinctions to compare Republicans and Democrats on these issues to more clearly specify how they differ, in terms of religion, environmental concern, and other factors. In particular, chapter 5 examines the possibility that Republican or Democrat identities explain *away* the religion–environment connection by comparing models including only Republicans (and those who lean Republican) to models including only Democrats (and those who lean Democrat). In all other models, I controlled for political party to ensure that I am not capturing some effect of political ideology rather than religious group identity in predicting environmental concern. If there is a consistent negative relationship between Republicans and environmental concern, and a consistent positive relationship between Democrats and environmental concern, then this suggests that the religious motivation is partly indirect (Type 2) rather than direct (Type 1), driven by political commitments rather than cultural heritage. People who would already be expected to be more environmentally concerned on average, in fact, are net of the effect of religion.

I also included *demographic* and *geographic* variables. Sociologists have long been interested in how race, class, gender, educational, and geographic differences affect other aspects of people's lives. As a sociologist, it seemed likely that these differences affect religion, and levels of environmental concern, as well. In chapter 5, I detailed some of the ways these differences matter when it comes to the religion–environment connection, and how they offer a more complete picture of the relationships described elsewhere in this book. For now, I note that I included sex (male or female), race (measured black, white, or other race), perceived income (below average, average, or above average income), and education (highest year of school completed, 0–20). To capture geography, I used a measure of region and a measure of whether people live in urban or rural areas based on population density. These are also part of determining whether there are Type 2 (indirect) or Type 1 (direct) motives. If motives are indirect, then, again, groups that would already be expected to be environmentally concerned would be, net of religion.

A CRASH COURSE IN MODEL-BUILDING

The word *regression* probably sounds familiar to those with a background in statistics of some kind. For those without such a background, the great thing about regression is that it's something everyone who took an algebra course in middle school or high school already knows how to do. Somewhere along the way, people are likely to have learned a simple equation:

$$y = mx + b$$

The solution to this equation, rather than being a single number, is plotted on a line, where the relationship between y and x depends on the values of m and b. Let's flip this around, so that it reflects the way in which social scientists do it:

$$y = a + bx$$

Here, as with the other equation, the value of y (the *outcome*) is dependent on the values of a (the *y-intercept*), x (a *predictor*), and b (the *slope*). Let's assume, for example, that $a=1$ and $b=2$. It makes sense, then, that if $x=0$ then $y=1$; this is what a represents, or the intercept: it is the value of y when $x=0$. If $x=1$, then $y = 1 + 2(1)$, or $y=3$. In other words, b is the *slope*—it is how much y changes every time x changes by 1. If $y =1 + 2x$, then y is 1 when x is 0, and y changes by 2 every time x changes by 1, because $b=2$. This means that when $x=2$, $y=5$, or when $x=3$, $y=7$, and so on. Now, the standard regression equation:

$$\hat{y} = b_0 + b_1 X_1 + b_2 X_2 \ldots + e$$

Though it is possible to picture that equation from Algebra I, with its single intercept and slope, as a straight line on a two-dimensional surface, each additional predictor x in regression is its own slope and adds another dimension to the equation. In other words, trying to picture an equation with a lot of different slopes requires thinking in more than three dimensions, and will probably just give you a headache. But the math works.

The intercept in this more complicated equation is still the value of y when all those other x's are zero. To compare religious groups' (x's) levels of environmental concern (y), I chose a *reference* category: *none,* or the religiously unaffiliated. The birth cohort variable as well as all those controls are also x's that go on the right-hand side of the equation. Environmental concern, because it's measured in yes ($y=1$) or no ($y=0$) terms, becomes a change in probability for each predictor. That looks like this:

$$p(y=1) = b_0 + b_1 x_1 + b_2 x_2 \ldots + e$$

Probabilities are easy to work with, because they can be translated into percentages. A probability of .741, for example, means there is a model-predicted 74.1% chance of something happening (and a probability of 1-.741=.259, a 25.9% chance of it not happening). There are at least two problems with this model: the error (e) isn't very reliable (see Mood 2010), and it can predict impossible outcomes (less than 0 or greater than 1). Many quantitative methodologists advise against using it for these reasons (see Hoffman 2004, 45–6). Given that this book is intended to be accessible to a broader educated audience, I'm going to report percentages based on changes in probability, and because most of them aren't too close to 0 or 1, this should be ok (see Hellevik 2009). For the error, and to check to make sure things are working like they should, I also ran and compared some more complicated models (see Szrot 2019), reporting the errors using *p-values:* $* p < .05$, $** p < .01$, $*** p < .001$. The lower the *p-value* is, the more asterisks it gets, and the more significant the relationship is (the more likely it is a "signal," or a meaningful finding, rather than "noise" or something that is statistically random). I have used n/s as an abbreviation for cases when the religious group is not significantly different from the unaffiliated. For more on the advanced models used here (called *binary logistic regression* for those interested), principles are detailed elsewhere for interested readers (see Hoffman 2004, 46–54).

So far, the regression equations noted estimate separate slopes for *birth cohort* and *religious group identity*. That is, each was a predictor (x) that predicted the outcome (y, or environmental concern). The research question, however, was how do *religious groups change over time?* This means religious groups might *change differently* across birth cohorts. To simplify, so far, the basic model is

$$p(y=1) = b_{intercept} + b_{relig.} x_1 + b_{cohort} x_2 \ldots + e$$

In order to compare how religious groups changed over time, I added another term, an *interaction effect,* to the model, so that it became

$$p(y=1) = b_{intercept} + b_{relig.} x_1 + b_{cohort} x_2 + b_{relig*cohort} x_3 \ldots + e$$

This created two different kinds of effects. The intercept is still the percent that express environmental concern when the other predictors are all zero.

The "*b*" for religion becomes the slope for religion at cohort zero, and the "*b*" for cohort becomes the slope for cohort for an unaffiliated person (recall this is the reference group). That added relig*cohort term is called an *interaction effect:* it allows the cohort slope to be different for each religious group. Using interaction effects, different rates of change across different religious groups could be captured and compared. It is possible to test lots of interaction effects in any model, though that gets messy fast, and change among religious groups across birth cohorts was the primary effect of interest for this study. Again, models are simplifications, or useful stories told with numbers; it is not expected that any model will be perfect, only that it will improve knowledge of existing trends.

What if cohorts did not change *linearly,* that is, they did not change in a straight line? There are many ways that cohorts might change over time that are not straight lines, but one of the simplest *nonlinear* models involves adding yet another term:

$$p(y=1) = b_{intercept} + b_{relig.}x_1 + b_{cohort}x_2 + b_{relig*cohort}x_3 + b_{cohort*cohort}x_4 \ldots + e$$

Early statistical tests found that this model was more accurate. Basically, this means that environmental concern tended to increase with more recent birth cohorts, but increased at a slower rate. The exact rate of change depended on the religious group (remember the role of the interaction effect). Interactions were tested with this *cohort-squared* term but did not improve the models. This means that all religious groups were expected to follow a similar decelerating positive trend (though their individual intercepts and slopes differed). For a thorough, step-by-step explanation as to how to interpret interaction effects in regression models, see L. Hoffman (2015, 41–78).

There are three ways things can change over time. Cohort analysis is just one. It is the most frequently used type of model in the rest of this book, as it fits with the theoretical assumptions and research question that animated the research project on which it is based, but I also compared this cohort analysis to a model which separated the effects of year from the effects of age—a *multilevel* model. This is a more advanced type of regression model. As I worry that the reader who does not have a "passion for statistics" might already be yawning, I will point the interested reader to a detailed guide on multilevel models. I highly recommend the aforementioned work by Lesa Hoffman (2015).

These models were used near the end of chapter 4, comparing *year effects* and *age effects* to *cohort effects* to see where they agreed, and disagreed, in terms of what's happening. They're ways to keep me honest. Operating on a *falsifiability* criterion (see Popper 1962), I see the point of conducting research as not to prove a "pet theory" but to test the many ways in which it might be wrong. That meant also looking more closely at gender, social class, race, and political party as potentially explaining—or explaining away—the trends in environmental concern across religious groups over time. Race, religion, and political party were examined together because of the historical significance of the relationship between race, religion, and politics in the U.S. (see Emerson and Smith 2000; Jones 2016; Shelton and Emerson 2012). Put another way, parts of chapter 4 as well as chapter 5 were written largely as an effort to prove myself wrong. Though I don't prove myself wrong (spoiler alert), these different approaches offer insights and a few surprises that complicate the religion–environment connection and require some explanation.

CHAPTER SUMMARY: THE STAGE IS SET

This chapter, spanning both concepts and methods, sets the stage for the rest of the book. I want to provide a clear and concise summary and recap before moving on, especially highlighting how these concepts and methods can be used to directly address the religion–environment connection. In particular, what are the specific *research questions* that are addressed in each chapter, and how were these questions answered? This chapter summary is written to provide a road map to the rest of this work.

The first issue raised was how to know whether and to what extent religion, in fact, motivates environmental concern. To that end, I developed three motives that can be examined in the rest of the book: Type 1 motive, in which religion directly motivates environmental concern; Type 2 motive, an indirect link between religion and environmental concern; Type 3 motive, a link between religion and environmental concern not visible to those who are motivated by it. Second, I considered *habitus* as a personal set of "second-nature" beliefs and behaviors that are shaped by early childhood influence and endure, to some degree, over the course of a lifetime. This is in contrast to *reflexivity,* or the ability to be self-reflective, responding to changing conditions—in particular, I am interested in the habitus of *individual persons* as well as the reflexivity of *religious groups over time.* Finally, I briefly described how the model-building process works and why it was conducted as it was for the purposes of the next three chapters.

Chapter 3 compares religious *upbringing* to religious *dis/affiliation.* If environmental concern is linked to religious upbringing through habitus, then how are people who remain in the religion of their upbringing different from people who leave? This chapter briefly addresses Type 1 motives, but is focused on the ways in which habitus shapes individual attitudes toward the environment more indirectly. If the link is indirect (Type 2), then there should not be much difference between religious upbringing and adult religiosity in terms of environmental concern. Other factors, such as political party, education, gender, race, and birth cohort, should play a bigger role. That is, if religion is less a motivator than part of a broader set of reasons for environmental concern (arrived at through largely "secular" reasoning processes), then groups of people who would already be expected to be environmentally concerned (per the Buttel model, see Buttel 1979) will remain so. If habitus is durable, then even those who disaffiliate should have similar levels of environmental concern to those of the same religious upbringing. This may be an example of Type 3, or invisible, motive—people may, on average, not even be aware of these similarities because the root of this is second-nature, and found in early childhood. These possibilities are not mutually exclusive.

Chapter 4, which brings in the intergenerational component (cohort effects), and also looks at the role of age and year, compares religious *groups over time*. The question here: how and why have different religious groups changed over time, on average, in terms of environmental concern? In chapter 4, Type 1 (direct) versus Type 2 (indirect) motivations can be examined further by testing "closeness to" one's religion further as well as some of the background factors associated with environmental concern. Again, these possibilities are not mutually exclusive. Drawing on the results of chapters 3 and 4, a summary as to how and why environmental concern is connected to religious identity, as well as the more likely types of motivation and their relationship to both habitus and reflexivity, is offered at the end of chapter 4.

Chapter 5 uses the same intergenerational approach that was introduced in chapter 4, but does so in order to challenge the findings from chapters 3 and 4. In particular, how and why are women and men linked differently to both religion and environmental concern? How and why are low-, middle-, and high-income people linked differently to both religion and environmental concern? How and why does the religion–environment connection differ by political party and race? Building on the summary at the end of chapter 4, this chapter examines what broader sociological factors may be driving the religion–environment connection based on the results of these models. That is, how might gender, social class, and racial inequalities, as well as political divides, have shaped, or continue to shape, the religion–environment connection?

Chapter 6 concludes by zooming out further, addressing these issues in more detail. The goal of chapter 6 is to summarize the results and explain how these results fit into some of the "bigger-picture" cultural, political, and economic shifts and possibilities. And in this bigger picture, where does religion fit, and what role might religious persons and institutions play in addressing environmental issues in the future based on the results of this analysis? This is not merely an exercise in curiosity and speculation, but an effort to address the relationship between religion and science, human beings and the rest of the cosmos—how it has changed, and how and why it may change even more dramatically in the future.

Chapter 3

Religious Upbringing, Disaffiliation, Environmental Concern

This seems like a good place to ask: how did you become *you*? It's one of the most basic sociological questions, and the answer, fundamentally, involves *interactions with other people*. Parents and caregivers make decisions about how to raise a child before birth, launching into motion all kinds of expectations about what kind of person their child would be. Families have ideas about what it means to be a part of the community and culture, why these are good and right ways of living in the world, and how to pass them on. They in turn learned those ideas from their own childhood, and from the institutions and cultural context of their own society. People are *socialized* into a world in which certain ideas and expectations take shape, and are passed on, across generations. And religion is typically part of this process, as well: being raised Catholic, I was baptized in infancy, becoming a member of the church, and taking on a variety of new rules, rituals, rites, and expectations that became a part of life. Perhaps you were raised in a religion as well, which had different patterns of socialization, different rites and rituals, or perhaps in no religion at all. If I had been raised in a different place, at a different time, by different parents, in a different religion (or no religion at all), then I would be a very different person.

Family and religion can be easily thought of as institutions that human beings are "born into": they shape the course of our lives in multiple profound ways, from the beginning. Of course, there is a lot of variation across place and time as far as what families look like, as well as what religion consists of, but both are fairly ubiquitous. Considering the influence of family, and of religion, does not mean stopping with the things parents and caregivers teach. They learned those things from somewhere, as well; they needed other human beings to teach them how to be human, and had parents and caregivers and religion too. Worldviews are not simply a matter of personal choice, spewing fully formed from one mind alone. They are the result of centuries of human endeavor across many different levels of society. More specifically, sociologist of religion Peter Berger (1967) argued that humans build social reality by absorbing the expectations of the society into which they are born, and then reinforcing those expectations in turn. In the context of religion, a "sacred canopy," or a coherent religious worldview, with specific rules, ethos, and cultural norms embedded within it, is taken on at an early age, and survives to be reinforced and passed on in adulthood.

What did Grover Cleveland, William Henry Harrison, Theodore Roosevelt, and Woodrow Wilson have in common with John Denver and Rachel Carson? Four of them were presidents of the U.S. during what has come to be called the Progressive Era; one was a folk singer famous for drawing on "nature themes" in his work, and one was an ecologist who sounded the warning on pesticides, in many ways catalyzing the modern environmental movement. All were concerned about the environment, and all were raised Presbyterian (see Stoll 2015, 191, 196–7, 277–82). The difference, beyond the first four being presidents, is that both Carson and Denver were lapsed Presbyterians, but all could be thought of as what sociologist Max Weber famously called "social carriers" (see Weber 2011, 48–9), or people who carry forward elements of a historical ethic (even if their commitments to the religious basis for that ethic fade). In describing Weber's argument in *The Protestant Ethic and the Spirit of Capitalism*, sociologist Stephen Kalberg argued: "Weber's analysis of how the Protestant ethic survives—in secularized guise as a spirit of capitalism carried by families, schools, and civic associations—offers a vivid illustration of the way in which values and ideas from the past for him endure as legacies and influence the present" (see Weber 2011, 48).

Putting these big sociological and historical ideas into the context of the current set of questions: *religious upbringing is an important predictor of any attitude expected to be linked to religion, at least as important as a person's adult religious affiliation.* It also follows that the religious group, culture, and worldview into which people are born and raised are likely to continue affecting them, even if they leave the religion of their parents in adolescence or adulthood. This chapter focuses on two overlooked dynamics that shed light on the religion–environment connection. First, how does religious *upbringing* affect environmental concern? That is, how and why is it different in its effects from simply measuring adult religious affiliation? Second, what effects does religious disaffiliation have on environmental attitudes relative to persons who remain religiously affiliated, and why? If there is a shared Presbyterian ethic that animated Progressive era conservationist presidents, ecologically minded folk singers, and scientists challenging the wisdom and morality of widespread pesticide use, then perhaps such an ethic can be found more broadly in the U.S., and can be connected back to the distinctiveness of religious upbringing.

THOSE WHO STAY AND THE EX'S:
RELIGIOUS MOTIVES, REVISITED

Before jumping in, I want to briefly revisit the concept of habitus, this time more deliberately from the "micro-level," the level of the person. Again, and without getting too technical, *habitus* refers to a package of things that we each learn and internalize from the surrounding culture (including family and religion), often without being consciously aware of it. It's possible to think of early life as a process of copying a "rule book" from parents, caregivers, and others who model the expected and accepted ways of being a person in a cultural context. However, people aren't "blank slates," passively waiting society's inscription. Human beings are living, dynamic organisms. The first time a two-year-old utters the seemingly magical syllable *No,* it becomes clear that this process of internalizing a "rule book" is far from perfect.

For Bourdieu (1993, 5), *habitus* arises in a specific cultural *field,* in which this rule book takes on "law-like" qualities (continuing my metaphor). It's not illegal for me to show up to a wedding dressed in my gym clothes, eat spaghetti with my hands at a fancy restaurant, or teach one of my classes while lying on the floor—it's just that *people don't do that.* As children learn "the rules," they also begin to learn what rules can be bent, or broken, and in what contexts. Adults are a result of the ongoing dynamic tension between self and society, obeying, questioning, bending, and breaking rules, and shaping both selves and our social worlds in the process.

Putting *habitus* together with the idea of *socialization* at the beginning of this chapter, it is possible that attitudes toward the environment, insofar as they are shaped by religion, are introduced and internalized at an early age. In fact, it is not necessarily the religious institution alone that cultivates this habitus. For children, having experiences in the context of faith-based organizations and groups, such as participating in Scouts, camping trips, or nature hikes, may be more effective at developing a "greener" habitus than listening to a sermon about the environment during a church service. This, again, would suggest the possibility of Type 2 (instrumental) and Type 3 (invisible) religious motives—environmental concern may arise out of the context of religious upbringing and interaction with religious organizations, but is not a direct consequence of specific religious teachings. However, it is also the case (as will be discussed further in the next chapter) that religious organizations have a long history of engaging with environmental issues. Religious groups can, and often do, also *respond to* environmental concern through religious messaging that has arisen in the context of the surrounding society, through scientists, educators, and advocates.

Habitus also helps to explain how a Type 3, or invisible, motive is possible, and why it may occur. It is possible that religion influences environmental concern in ways that we are not consciously aware of. I think about my Catholic upbringing, and how many things that I didn't even realize I did differently because of it. Habitus shapes the way we think about the world, see ourselves, and conduct ourselves. Consider the closeness of the word habitus to a root—*habit*—human beings do a lot of things habitually, without giving them long or sustained consideration. It's probably a good thing, because it frees up attention to learn and do other things, as well as planning what's next. It also means that a lot of the results of socialization are not really visible to the person acting on them. It takes time and effort to *notice*. Indeed, one way to test whether an invisible motive is present is by comparing people who are religious to people who leave the church of their upbringing. I refer to them henceforth as people who *Stay* and *Ex's*, respectively.

A great deal of work has gone into trying to make sense of why some people leave religion, and why others stay. At the micro-level, Ex's are different from those who stay in terms of personality, cognitive styles, and ideological frameworks, differences which might also come from early childhood environments or even heritable traits (Galen 2014). Zooming out a bit, disaffiliation is more likely when a person's teenage social networks are less religiously engaged (Pearce and Denton 2011; Smith and Snell 2009). Moving upward to the institutional level, religious groups themselves can play a role. By excluding certain behaviors and identities, and enforcing certain moral teachings, they can foster *cognitive dissonance*, or internal tensions between incompatible beliefs and attitudes, leading adolescents and emerging adults to leave the religion of their upbringing and perhaps develop strong suspicions toward organized religion in general (Barry and Abo-Zena 2014; Public Religion Research Institute 2012). Some research suggests that stricter churches may be *better* able to retain membership because they reinforce social networks populated by more religious, and more religiously engaged, persons (Szrot and Collins 2019). In other words, the decision to stay, or leave, is heavily shaped by social factors. However, given that religion is learned and internalized from an early age, comparing those who remain religiously engaged to those who leave the religion of their upbringing offers a novel way to look at how religion may motivate environmental concern.

The models on which this chapter is based are fairly straightforward, and the model-building process can also illuminate exactly how religious upbringing and disaffiliation work to shape environmental concern. Model-building ultimately is both art and a science. There are all kinds of questions that can be answered by the process of model-building itself, because models respond with mathematical precision to the questions model-builders put to them. That is, models tell model-builders whether adding a variable makes the model *better*, or whether taking a variable out makes the model *worse*. In this case, this means better, or worse, at predicting environmental concern. The general goal is to make the model both *efficient* and *parsimonious*—models should explain as much about how religious upbringing and disaffiliation are related to environmental concern as possible with as a few variables as possible, based on the assumptions that went into building it and the questions one is trying to answer. This involves an ongoing process of negotiation: adding and subtracting variables, and subjecting the model to various tests. If I want to know, for example, whether people who leave religion differ in environmental concern depending on the religious group they were raised in, I can test that. If I want to know whether people who left religion differ in environmental concern based on when they were born (in this case, the birth cohort or generation they were born into), I can test that too. And I did. The answer to both questions was *no*.

This means that, even though the bigger reasons people *Stay* and the reasons people become *Ex's* are complicated, it is disaffiliation *per se* affects environmental concern. Baptists, Methodists, Catholics, and Buddhists who leave the religion in which they were brought up are affected similarly in terms of environmental concern by that decision. The effect of being an "Ex" is also not *conditional* on the generation into which a person was born—people born before 1905 and people born after 1980 who leave religion are affected similarly in terms of environmental concern. Taken together, this suggests cultural similarities among religiously unaffiliated adults, which are visited at the end of this chapter. This is also good news as far as the table of numbers that I'm about to present: they are more straightforward than the tables in the next two chapters.

"STAY" AND "EX," PATTERNS AND MOTIVES

Table 3.1 details how religious upbringing and disaffiliation shape levels of environmental concern across both variables (stewardship and conservation). The first column (*%Tot*) contains the "market share," or the percentage raised in that particular religious group. The second column (*%Ex*) also shows the rate of disaffiliation between the early 1970s and the mid-2010s *overall*. Almost one in three U.S.-Americans (29%) was raised Catholic, and fully 10 percent of those raised Catholic disaffiliated sometime after age 16. Baptists, making up almost a quarter of the religious market (23%), had lowest levels of disaffiliation overall—just 6 percent. There are some reasons to suspect that stricter religious groups do have an easier time retaining memberships

Table 3.1   **Percent Expressing Environmental Concern by Upbringing, Disaffiliation**

Upbringing	Market Share		% Stewardship			% Conservation		
	%Tot	%Ex	Stay	Ex	Sig.	Stay	Ex	Sig.
Baptist	23	6	38	44	**	25	30	***
Methodist	11	7	36	42	*	23	28	*
Presbyterian	7	8	41	47	***	24	28	*
Lutheran	4	10	35	41	n/s	24	29	**
Episcopalian	2	12	43	49	***	28	33	***
Nondenominational	8	9	34	40	n/s	21	25	n/s
Fundamentalist Prot.	2	7	34	40	n/s	23	27	n/s
Moderate Protestant	1	10	32	38	n/s	21	25	n/s
Liberal Protestant	3	15	42	48	**	24	28	n/s
Catholic	29	10	36	42	*	23	27	n/s
Jewish	2	10	42	48	***	22	26	*
Other Religion	3	17	33	38	n/s	22	26	n/s
None (Reference)	**5**	**62**	**39**			**24**		

Note: Total and Ex market share figures based on valid responses from full data set, $N = 56,085$. Stewardship $N = 34,143$, Conservation $N = 16,614$. Sig reports abbreviated: *** = high ($p < .001$), ** = moderate ($p < .01$), * = low ($p < .05$), n/s = not significantly different from those raised unaffiliated. Significance reported based on main upbringing coefficients, and standard errors based on binary logistic regression for more conservative results. "None as adult" disaffiliation coefficient high sig. in both models.

Controls: Birth Cohort (0–6) and Cohort², Attend Religious Services Weekly or More, High Confidence in Scientific Community, High Confidence in Organized Religion, Education, Sex, Race, income, Region, Size of Town/City, Political Party, Feelings about the Bible (Conservation model only).

even when breaking down religious groups by these historical denominations (Finke and Stark 2007; Iannaccone 1994). This is probably because they are able to build social networks that reinforce their beliefs (see Szrot and Collins 2019), and this is probably why *other religion*, an umbrella group for those who belong to religious groups that constitute a tiny fraction of the total "market share," has the highest percentage of *Ex's*, over one in six. People in smaller religious groups, on average, retain contact with fewer people who share and can reinforce their beliefs, leading to higher levels of disaffiliation in adolescence and early adulthood. *None* serves as a reference group, another "umbrella category" including everyone who identifies as religiously unaffiliated. Only 5 percent of the total population were raised without any religious affiliation. More than six in ten (62%) of religiously unaffiliated adults polled between 1973 and 2014 were raised in a religion. Among those adults with no religious affiliation, the majority were raised in a religious group.

Turning to the findings themselves, the *Stay* column shows that stewardship levels vary across groups, with highest levels among liberal other Protestants, Episcopalians, Presbyterians, and Jewish persons. These groups tend to be more theologically liberal and culturally progressive (rather than moderate or fundamentalist/culturally orthodox), and Presbyterians have a long history of environmental engagement. Of the unaffiliated who were raised unaffiliated, almost four in ten (39%) expressed stewardship. This means that Episcopalians, liberal Protestants, Presbyterians, and Jewish persons who *Stay* expressed higher levels of stewardship than the unaffiliated who were raised unaffiliated.

Interestingly, the highest levels of stewardship overall tend to be found among those persons who were raised religious and disaffiliated later in life, the *Ex's.* There is a six-percentage-point increase in stewardship overall among the Ex's relative to those who Stay. And as noted previously, the model "told" me during construction that the increase is dependent neither on the religious group nor on the birth cohort. However, it is people raised in "theologically liberal" groups—Presbyterians, Episcopalians, liberal other Protestants, and Jewish persons—who later disaffiliated that are most likely to express stewardship. People raised in more moderate religious backgrounds, such as Methodists and Catholics, as well as those raised as largely theologically fundamentalist Baptists, but who disaffiliated later in life, express stewardship at somewhat higher rates than those who are unaffiliated and were raised unaffiliated. These results hold even when adding all controls into the model, as listed at the bottom of table 3.1, but for some groups, the difference is not statistically significant (n/s).

Turning to conservation, there are some significant differences, largely among historical Protestant groups, but many Protestant groups are generally fairly similar to the unaffiliated. However, the *Ex's* in all six significant groups express higher levels of conservation than the unaffiliated. Overall, four-percentage-point increases in conservation are found among those who identify as unaffiliated as adults, but again, the highest levels are among those coming from religious (specifically historical Protestant denominations) backgrounds. Interestingly, however, these results do not line up with theological or cultural stances of these groups. Baptists tend to be more theologically fundamentalist and culturally orthodox, but they express conservation at a higher rate than any other group except for Episcopalians. Both groups express conservation at higher levels than the unaffiliated. Presbyterians, Lutherans, and liberal Protestants express similar levels of conservation to the unaffiliated. Again, as with stewardship, the highest levels of conservation are found among those raised religious, who disaffiliated later in life.

How does religion motivate environmental concern, then? Type 1 motive, or a direct link between religious identity and environmental concern, is unlikely. Not only was religious service attendance significantly negatively related to both types of environmental concern in the original research, but disaffiliating as an adult is linked to *higher* levels of environmental concern on both measures. Neither of these would be expected if religious upbringing was directly related to environmental concern. Type 2 motive, or instrumental relationships between religion and environmental concern, is likely part of the story. Highest levels of environmental concern tend to be found among those who are Democrats or Independents politically, live in more urban areas/regions, the more highly educated, and younger people (for full details, see Szrot 2019). But this explanation is also incomplete: if people are bringing environmental issues into religion from outside, then why are the highest levels found among the *Ex's*?

Based on these findings, what is happening in terms of religious upbringing and environmental concern is probably best thought of as a Type 3, or *invisible*, motive. Religious upbringing, particularly in religious groups with a history of engaging with environmental issues (see Yaple 1982), is connected to higher levels of environmental concern, but this is likely more closely related to the deeper religious roots of environmentalism, and their long-standing relationship to U.S. culture (see Berry 2015; Stoll 2015). In other words, people raised in certain historical religious groups are more likely to develop a "greener" *habitus* from an early age in connection with nature outings, Scouting, and other activities that are not overtly religious *per se*, but are connected to religious organizations through the social networks in which parents and children within religious institutions tend to more often participate.

Organized religion can cultivate higher levels of environmental concern in those with a religious upbringing through what sociologists have called *bridging social capital*: membership in one organization (in this case, organized religion) "builds bridges" between persons and organizations, producing new opportunities for engagement and interaction. Religion "builds a bridge" to activities, institutions, and social networks that allow religious youth to constructively engage with nature, in turn inspiring greater environmental concern in adulthood. As noted by political scientists Pippa Norris and Ronald Inglehart (2011), "Bridging networks are thought to foster the conditions for collaboration, coordination, and cooperation to create collective goods" (181). In his work *Bowling Alone*, sociologist Robert Putnam (2000) argues: "Faith communities in which people worship together are arguably the single most important repository of social capital in America" (66). Put simply, some religious institutions foster higher levels of environmental concern which "rubs off" indirectly during childhood socialization and is carried forward into adulthood.

This is half an explanation. That churches and religious institutions are important bridges to other social networks and organizations, for both adults and youth, does not explain why the *highest* levels are found among those who leave organized religion altogether. It is generally true that people raised in more theologically liberal religious groups are a bit more likely to disaffiliate, but these religious groups make up a small market share. It's also likely that people leave organized religion because of disagreements about values and priorities, but it isn't really plausible that people are leaving churches in large numbers because religious organizations don't care enough about the environment. Research shows that regular and irregular religious service attenders participate in conservation, environment, and animal rights groups at roughly equal levels, with slightly *higher* participation among those who attend religious services weekly or more (Norris and Inglehart 2011, 190). If religious people want to get involved in such organizations, they actually have *more*, rather than fewer, opportunities to do so via faith-based social networks.

It is also interesting that disaffiliating, *per se*, rather than disaffiliating from a particular religious group, is linked to an increase in environmental concern. This suggests that people who leave organized religion are similar to one another in ways that *also* steer them toward greater levels of environmental concern. That is, unaffiliated adults may be culturally similar to one another, as are other religious groups, in ways that tend to raise existing levels of environmental concern among those who have disaffiliated. Understanding more about unaffiliated adults as a group should help to explain why disaffiliation has a significant positive effect on environmental concern on both measures and across all groups.

ENVIRONMENTAL CONCERN
AND THE UNAFFILIATED

As a group, the unaffiliated are often a bit of a mystery. Exactly what does it mean to be "religiously unaffiliated"? This is a "big tent," one might say, containing people from many different religious backgrounds, with a lot of diversity and depth in beliefs and practices (see Bellah et al. 1996). As noted above, over 60 percent of people in this group were raised in some organized religion but dropped out sometime after age 16. There aren't a lot of scholars actively and systematically studying "nonbelief" from a sociological perspective (noteworthy exceptions include Baggett 2019; Zuckerman 2012, 2014). It is worth asking in this context what it means to be religious in the first place. In the U.S., for example, what it means to be "religious" is commonly defined in terms of belonging to a typically Judeo-Christian, but possibly Muslim, Hindu, Buddhist, Taoist, or other large global religious group. There are three challenges when examining the "nones": first, who are the unaffiliated, as a group? Second, how do they differ culturally from the rest of the U.S. in general, and how do these differences link to higher levels of environmental concern (especially among the Ex's)? Third, how do differences among the religiously unaffiliated in terms of environmental concern map onto the questions raised in this chapter so far? After examining the unaffiliated more systematically, I can return to the bigger questions of upbringing and disaf-filiation that animate this chapter, and the book as a whole.

Figure 3.1 shows how the unaffiliated differ from the U.S. population as a whole. Only around one in five of the unaffiliated identify as or lean Republican (compared to nearly 35% of the U.S.). The unaffiliated are more likely to live in the western U.S., are more urban, younger, and less likely

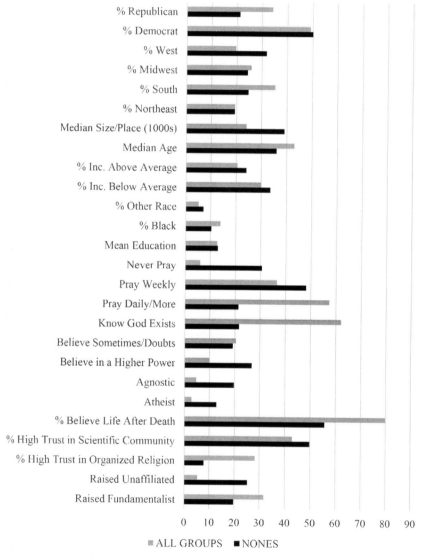

Figure 3.1   A Snapshot of the Unaffiliated.

to be middle class or Black. They have higher levels of trust in the scientific community, much lower levels of trust in organized religion, are more likely to be raised unaffiliated, and are less likely to be raised in a fundamentalist religious group (recall that stricter religious groups may be better at retaining membership). Overall, they are slightly more educated than the general public. Placed in the context of Hunter's (1991) "culture wars" thesis, the characteristics of the unaffiliated strongly suggest that they are, as a group, *culturally progressive* rather than *culturally orthodox*.

Perhaps these findings are not particularly surprising, overall. What is more interesting, I think, are the ways in which the unaffiliated compare to the general public (all groups) in terms of measures of "religious" beliefs and acts. First, there is prayer, a common practice across many different religious groups. Only about 5 percent of U.S.-Americans surveyed here report never praying, when compared to almost a third of the unaffiliated. Praying weekly, the gap shrinks quite a bit, with almost half of the "nones" praying weekly or infrequently (compared to a little over a third of the U.S. public as a whole). Daily prayer is reported by well over half of U.S.-Americans, but only about 22 percent of the "nones." In other words, the religiously unaffiliated as a group are less likely to pray, and less likely to pray daily, but they are actually *more likely* to pray weekly. Combined, about seven in ten unaffiliated persons pray at least weekly. Recall that over six in ten unaffiliated persons were raised religious.

Belief in God is not universally shared by all religions, but is definitely a staple belief among the majority of U.S. religious cultures. The General Social Survey also makes it possible to account for variations in belief in God—rather than a simple "yes" or "no," their measures account for levels of certainty or uncertainty, adding depth and nuance. Over 60 percent of U.S.-Americans (and over 20 percent of the unaffiliated) claim to *know God exists*. The unaffiliated are very similar to the general public in terms of those who *believe sometimes or have doubts*, and are more likely than the general public to believe in a nonspecific higher power. Only 20% of the unaffiliated identify as agnostics (persons who believe there is no way to know for sure, one way or another, if God exists) compared to about 5 percent of the general public, and about 13% of the unaffiliated are atheists (persons who do not believe in God) compared to about 3 percent of the general public. Again, the unaffiliated are less likely to believe in God, or a higher power, than the general public, but about two-thirds have some belief in God (are not agnostics or atheists). Recall that this is close to the percentage of the unaffiliated who pray at least weekly, as well as the percentage of the unaffiliated who were raised religious.

Finally, there is belief in life after death. As with belief in God, belief in an afterlife is not universal among all religions, but it is a key component of many U.S. religious groups. Fully 80% of U.S.-Americans believe in life after death, but over half the unaffiliated (nearly 60%) also believe similarly. So, *who are the unaffiliated as a group?* Over 60 percent were raised religious, seven in ten pray, two-thirds believe in a god or higher power, and almost 60 percent believe in life after death. It may be difficult to pin down exactly what it means to be religious, but a *fully secular* person would be expected to never pray, identify as agnostic or atheist, and not believe in life after death. Only a minority of the unaffiliated, fewer than three in ten, actually fit into this category. Though the unaffiliated are significantly different from (and less religious than) the general public, they are not, by and large, fully secular.

It hardly seems coincidental that the percentage of the unaffiliated who pray, believe in a God or higher power, believe in life after death, and were raised religious are all within a few percentage points of one another: between 60 percent and 70 percent. I do not claim that these are the *exact same* people. There are people who are fully secular who were raised religious, and people who have adopted some religious beliefs and practices even though they were raised unaffiliated. However, there is enough statistical overlap, in terms of religious upbringing and religious beliefs/practices, to suggest that a significant minority of unaffiliated people continue to hold beliefs and practices learned from the religious *habitus* in which they were raised.

Again, highest levels of environmental concern were found among those who were raised religious (particularly in certain religious groups that are either theologically liberal and/or have a history of engaging with environmental issues), but disaffiliated sometime after age 16. If unaffiliated people carry forward certain practices and habits of mind that could be called a religious *habitus* even after they disaffiliate, then it is possible there are meaningful differences between those who adhere to these practices and those who do not. It is also possible that certain beliefs and practices among the unaffiliated are more closely linked to environmental concern. In other words, looking more closely at how these religious beliefs and practices influence environmental concern among the unaffiliated should further disentangle what specifically is driving higher levels of environmental concern among those who disaffiliate, specifically, and the religion–environment connection, in general.

Comparing the *fully secular* unaffiliated persons (who don't believe in God, don't pray, and don't believe in an afterlife) to others within the "big tent" of the unaffiliated, in terms of both stewardship and conservation, actually produced a few significant differences. It's noteworthy that the number of people in this sample is much smaller than the rest of the project, because the data for the variables used is not available every survey year between 1973 and 2014, and also because I separated out the unaffiliated (6 percent of the total) and looked at them separately as a group. I have not presented the full models here (the full models are available in Szrot 2019, 98), but there are a few interesting things to contribute to the story.

In terms of stewardship, those who pray daily are 12.7% more likely to express stewardship than those who never pray, and those who pray weekly are 10% more likely to express stewardship than those who never pray (both mid sig, or **). Additionally, trust in organized religion is negatively associated with stewardship even among the religiously unaffiliated, and trust in science is positively associated. Political party matters, but it matters less for the unaffiliated than it does for the general public. Race and gender are weakly associated with stewardship, with women holding higher levels and Blacks, lower levels. In conservation, there were a few significant relationships—only trust in science and identifying as a Republican were significantly (negatively) associated with conservation.

This means two things. On one hand, the fact that the unaffiliated really aren't that different from one another in terms of how religious beliefs and practices affect environmental concern suggests that being unaffiliated serves as a sort of "master identity" (see, for example, Ecklund et al. 2008, 1823) among adults when it comes to environmental concern. Disaffiliation *per se* positively affected environmental concern regardless of the religious group a person disaffiliated *from,* and the unaffiliated are fairly similar to one another overall in terms of environmental concern. On the other hand, the positive relationship between prayer and stewardship is noteworthy. I entertain two possible explanations. The first is that prayer, as a practice, is part of religious *habitus* carried over by unaffiliated persons who have either been exposed to religious ideas or have been religious themselves in the past (particularly in childhood). This agrees with the earlier result that the highest levels of environmental concern are found among the *Ex's.* The second possibility is that this is tapping into people who consider themselves "spiritual but not religious," and that prayer among the unaffiliated also points to a kind of sacred connection to "nature" among a subset of people who are spiritual but not religiously affiliated. The first explanation fits with the evidence, but I'm not ruling out the second. That is, it is likely that both being "spiritual not religious" and praying are connected to being raised religious and disaffiliating later in life, and higher environmental concern, in turn.

Overall, the unaffiliated are not that different from one another. However, there are a few indicators that a religious upbringing, once again, is linked to the highest levels of environmental concern among the unaffiliated. That this manifests itself in terms of prayer, and specifically with stewardship, is interesting. It raises some interesting questions about how spirituality among the unaffiliated might translate to higher levels of environmental concern. It also corroborates that religious upbringing, followed by disaffiliation later in life, is linked to highest levels of environmental concern overall.

CHAPTER SUMMARY: EXPLAINING
RELIGIOUS UPBRINGING, DISAFFILIATION,
AND ENVIRONMENTAL CONCERN

Returning to motives, is the religion–environment connection, at least in terms of upbringing and disaffiliation, best explained in terms of direct (Type 1), indirect (Type 2), or invisible (Type 3) religious motives? Type 1, or direct, motive can be safely ruled out. Attending religious services weekly or more, and confidence in organized religion, is negatively linked to environmental concern. If religion directly motivated environmental concern, then being "closer to" one's religion would positively influence environmental concern. Also, disaffiliating from religion has a consistent *positive* impact on environmental concern, meaning the highest levels of environmental concern are found among the *Ex's*.

It is equally possible that a direct religious motive could result in *anti-environmental* attitudes—that people are *less* environmentally concerned as a direct function of their religious, cultural, or theological worldviews. Looking at religious upbringing and disaffiliation makes clear that this is not the case, either. Though people who are "closer to" their religion are less environmentally concerned on average, people who are raised religious and stay religious tend to hold similar levels of environmental concern to those raised unaffiliated. In several cases, being raised religious also meant *higher* levels of environmental concern than being raised unaffiliated. Furthermore, it is those who were raised religious *and* disaffiliated later in life who have the highest levels of environmental concern overall on both measures. None of this supports a direct relationship between religion and environmental concern, either in positive or negative terms.

Perhaps there is a cultural, theological, or worldview difference driving these divides, such that people who are more *culturally progressive* are more likely to be environmentally concerned, and those who are *culturally orthodox* or *fundamentalist* are less so. As noted in chapter 2, many avenues of research have suggested that "strict" or "conservative" or "literal Bible believing" U.S.-American Protestants tend to hold lower levels of environmental concern than their counterparts (Eckberg and Blocker 1989; Guth et al. 1995; Hand and Van Liere 1984; Schwadel and Johnson 2017; Sherkat and Ellison 2007; Szrot 2019b). I speculated that this may be due to what Taylor (2007) calls resistance to "the immanent frame" or a tendency to prioritize human activity over divine intervention in terms of how reality is changed/shaped. When examining religious upbringing, support for these ideas was inconsistent. Being from a theologically liberal group was more closely linked to higher levels of stewardship. However, disaffiliation had a similar effect across all religious groups, whether fundamentalist/orthodox, moderate, or liberal/progressive. Some of the highest levels of conservation were found among Baptists, who are more theologically fundamentalist. Lowest levels of environmental concern were not necessarily found among more fundamentalist groups. In the conservation models, feelings about the Bible did not significantly predict conservation attitudes. Neither religious upbringing in general, nor a theologically fundamentalist upbringing specifically, leads directly to lower environmental concern. So much for Type 1 motives in the case of religious upbringing, but this does not fully rule out culture in terms of Type 2 motives.

If religion is not directly linked, perhaps there is an indirect link. Type 2, indirect, motive has some support. People who are already more likely to be environmentally concerned on average tend to share certain features/characteristics: higher trust in science and more highly educated (stewardship, not conservation), more likely to live in urban areas/regions, younger, less likely to vote Republican. Culturally, those who hold higher levels of environmental concern were referred to by Eckberg and Blocker (1996) as believers who tended to be more "nonfundamentalist" and to hold more "liberal" theological and cultural views (353). This holds true, to a degree—theologically liberal groups tend to hold higher levels of stewardship overall, along with the unaffiliated (but primarily disaffiliated from theologically liberal religious groups). Overall, *cultural progressivism* is linked to environmental concern, but is one among many factors, and differences between religious groups are still significant in several cases that do not line up with this expectation.

Again, it is possible that the indirect motive has a negative dimension: that those who would be *less* likely to be environmentally concerned would also be groups within the population who are less environmentally concerned on average, anyway. Republicans, those who are older, closer to organized religion, live in more rural areas/regions, and have less education and trust in science (stewardship in particular) are in fact less environmentally concerned on average. However, this ignores the mixed findings when it comes to religious groups. Theologically fundamentalist groups are not consistently less environmental concerned than theologically moderate groups. In some cases, largely theologically fundamentalist groups hold similar environmental concern to more liberal groups. That is, environmental concern, as measured through religious upbringing, is not as much a "casualty of the culture wars" as one might expect. It is not *just* the *culturally orthodox* who have lower levels of environmental concern on average.

In other words, there is some support for Type 2 motives here—that secular reasoning and broader cultural modes are bringing environmental concern in from the outside, but this explanation does not consistently capture the nuances of religious group identity, upbringing, and disaffiliation. Furthermore, there are many more questions that must be addressed in order to determine whether, and to what extent, environmental attitudes are being cultivated within, or outside of, religious institutions. This means zooming out to look at the broader historical trends and examining *changes over time* in environmental concern as a function of religious identity, which is the focus of chapter 4. For now, Type 2 motives remain of interest, but more needs to be done to establish how strong and consistent indirect motives are at work.

A Type 3 motive, that the way in which religion motivates environmental concern is *invisible* to the person being so motivated, is both intriguing and more broadly supported by the results here. Given the rejection of Type 1 motives, and the mixed support for Type 2 motives, it is likely not religious upbringing itself that directly drives environmental concern. Instead, it is the social and cultural opportunities related to religious upbringing that motivate higher levels of environmental concern. That is, children raised in an organized religion setting can access to various outdoor and educational events and opportunities through the faith-based social networks of parents or caregivers. By adulthood, people raised in a religious group, particularly one with a history of environmental concern or engagement (more on this in the next chapter), are likely to have had access to a variety of opportunities to appreciate, respect, and learn about the natural world, often (but not always) through a faith-based lens. Additionally, people raised in organized religion probably don't consciously consider the myriad little ways in which their understanding and appreciation of the natural world were cultivated in childhood through summer camps, Scouting, and other outdoor activities hosted by or accessible through their social networks or the social networks of parents/caregivers.

One of the primary reasons the unaffiliated tend to have higher levels of environmental concern in other research on the religion–environment connection (see chapter 1) is that most unaffiliated adults were raised in a religious group with higher levels of environmental concern. A solid majority of those who are religiously unaffiliated as adults *were raised religious*, and a majority of the unaffiliated still express various religious beliefs and behaviors. This, I suspect, is why prayer is positively associated with stewardship even among the unaffiliated, whereas other sets of beliefs aren't. Prayer is a religious *habitus* that is learned and internalized at an early age. It does not *determine* environmental concern, but arises in the same ways that respect and appreciation of nature may have been cultivated through youth outings accessed through faith-based social networks. Being raised without religious affiliation just does not offer the same such opportunities, though this may well change in the future.

Going beyond religious motives, there are, I think, two other likely factors that explain higher environmental concern among the *Ex's*, based on what other researchers in the sociology of religion have found. The first reflects broader trends in the U.S. and other wealthy nations toward more individualistic religious belief and practice, which have been well-studied by others (see Bellah et al. 1996; Lim et al. 2010; Roof and McKinney 1992; Voas 2009). That is, people who are, broadly speaking, "spiritual but not religious," who were raised in a religious household but as adults are neither fully secular nor part of an organized religion, may feel more connection to the natural world as a source of spiritual insight and inspiration. This could both explain why prayer is positively linked to environmental stewardship and why people who were raised religious but disaffiliated tend to have higher levels of environmental concern than those raised without religious affiliation. This remains a possibility that adds to, rather than replacing, the broader "social networks" explanations in this chapter.

Another possibility not yet discussed is that becoming an *Ex* is partially related to the ideological rather than spiritual content of U.S.-American religion, particularly since the 1980s. The flexibility and individualism that have become a hallmark of religion in the U.S. means that it is probably rare to leave religion explicitly because of a single issue on which they have come to be at odds with religious teaching. And as noted above, there are probably *more,* rather than fewer, opportunities to do environmental work within organized religion and faith-based social networks for those religious persons who are so inclined. However, people may leave organized religion because of larger-scale ideological *trends* in the U.S. cultural landscape. Specifically, it is possible that the being an *Ex* is linked to higher environmental concern because environmental issues have become an increasingly partisan political issue. Put simply, being a part of a church has become increasingly associated with being or leaning Republican in the U.S., and being a Republican is also consistently negatively associated with both measures of environmental concern. As noted by a sociologist of religion Mark Chaves (2011): "After 1990 people thought that saying you were religious was tantamount to saying you were a conservative Republican. So people who are not Republicans are now more likely to say they have no religion" (21). This is undoubtedly part of the explanation, but it is not a full explanation. The link between *theological* liberalism/fundamentalism, *cultural* progressivism/orthodoxy, and *political* liberalism/conservatism is hardly perfect, though there is significant overlap. It is also the case that *higher* levels of disaffiliation tend to be found among the more theologically liberal religious groups (and lower levels, among the more fundamentalist groups). To examine whether, and to what extent, this explains religious change and its effect on environmental concern means looking at broader historical trends across generations, as well as separating out religious and political factors. I undertake the broader historical analysis in chapter 4, and further pull apart political effects from cultural and religious factors shaping environmental concern in chapter 5.

Religious *habitus* includes opportunities to constructively engage with the environment, translating to higher levels of environmental concern, on average, in adulthood. At least part of the effect is invisible to those who are acting upon it. As with other kinds of habitus, and with culture more broadly, describing it is a bit like asking a fish to describe water (see Long 2011). That is, religion, as part of the cultural context in which people grow and mature, connects people to myriad beliefs and behaviors that ordinarily go unnoticed to those who hold them. A 38-year-old environmentalist may have trouble remembering how nature hikes with the Boy Scouts introduced in him wonder and joy at the natural world, and may never have been aware of how his parents met other parents at church through whom they got him involved in Scouting, and by extension, that nature hike.

It takes a degree of *reflexivity*, or self-reflection, to recognize how, and to what extent, culture shapes individual lives. At the micro-level, sociology enables those who understand and practice it to reveal what is taken for granted, to question what is second-nature, and to see the contours of the social world that shapes human lives. However, it is not simply people, but more importantly, institutions, that are self-reflective, responding to changing environments over time. How, and to what extent, do bigger historical shifts across generations and institutions correspond to, and explain, levels of environmental concern across religious groups? That is the focus of chapter 4.

Chapter 4

Religion and Environmental Concern, Intergenerationally

A story of how people develop environmental concern across a lifetime, and how this is related to religion, would be incomplete without addressing the larger historical trends in which these dynamics happen. The history of religion and environmental concern in the U.S. is so complex that maybe it makes more sense to speak of multiple, overlapping "histories" shaped by perceptions of the environment, and how human beings made sense of their relationship to it. The focus of this chapter is how to make sense of these histories at the intersection of religious groups and environmental concern. Accordingly, there are four major sections to this chapter. In the first, I briefly visit these interlocking histories and some of the tensions within them, as they manifest in terms of *the environment* and what it means to be *environmentally concerned*. Second, I examine intergenerational differences in environmental concern by religious groups and compare these results to both the story that emerged out of chapter 3. Third, I consider recent developments related to environmental change, examining how stewardship and conservation are related to age, year, and theological views. The goal of this third section is to test how the three different kinds of change over time—*age effects, cohort effects,* and *year effects*—are related to one another, and may overlap. In the final section of this chapter, I summarize the story of environmental concern and change over time as a function of religion, before moving into some more specifically sociological questions regarding race, class, gender, and politics in the next chapter.

In place of a "History" of environmental concern, a questionable "grand narrative" (see Lyotard 1985), I offer a sampling of competing and overlapping narratives, or stories, that are relevant to this story. They are incomplete, and can be contested, as any such story is, and can be. What is important is that they have been, and continue to be, influential. These stories overlap and conflict in multiple ways, underpinning the complicated historical vision of both *stewardship* and *conservation* as versions of environmental concern.

I start with a *conservation narrative* because it predates stewardship in many ways, and because a version of stewardship arises out of a certain conservation narrative. As European settlers began to arrive on the east coast of the Americas, they found *wilderness,* and saw in it sin and desolation. Life was undoubtedly difficult for these settlers. It is not difficult to imagine how, facing starvation and disease in a new land, they began to see nature as an enemy to be battled or a wild creature to be subdued. From this perspective, it was an act of "providence" to cultivate the land for human use and benefit. This vision of cultivation had led environmental historian Lynn White, Jr. (1967) to claim that Western Christianity was a uniquely human-centered view of nature. It has also been used to define Indigenous relationships to the land as "wasteful" and "improper," permitting areas occupied by First Peoples to be defined as "empty" (Purdy 2015; Sawyer 2004, 55). Put another way, sharply separating humans and nature gave license to subdue a hostile environment and use it for human needs. It also allowed an influx of colonial settlers to define *human* in ways that excluded the First Peoples from both rights to ancestral lands and full humanity.

This story assumes there is a gap between people and nature, between human spaces and natural spaces, defined in terms of *wilderness.* Wilderness is a *thing* that is separate from human beings. To *conserve wilderness,* then, means to value it for its own sake, and set it aside from human interference. To *not* conserve wilderness would imply that human beings have rights *over* nature as wilderness—to tame it, conquer it, and use it for their own ends. Some have cited a mandate from the Judeo-Christian tradition reflecting an opposition to conservation and license for human "dominion over" nature: "God created man in his image; in the divine image he created him; male and female he created them. God blessed them, saying: 'Be fertile and multiply; fill the earth and subdue it. Have dominion over the fish of the sea, the birds of the air, and all the living things that move on the earth'" (Genesis 1:27–29 [New American Bible]).

Today, versions of this story abound: the bumper sticker: "Are you an environmentalist, or do you work for a living?" (see White 1996); ambitious science-based proposals such as setting aside half the planet and its intact ecosystems as free of human interferences (see Wilson 2016); and in the ongoing and dubious service of the primitive-versus-civilized, the West-versus-the rest dichotomies in defining the human–nature relationship.

The roots of this story are deep, and can be traced back to an early "radical ethical protest against nature" in the context of Western civilization. This protest emerged out of Zoroastrianism, as founded in present-day Iran in the first century BCE. A dualism, cleaving human from nature, and good from evil, ultimately provided fertile theological ground for a worldview which sundered divine from human—and nature. In this cosmological view, nature could no longer be invoked as a criterion of right or wrong (Campbell 1986, 39, 87–9). Some would place this development at the door of a period called the Axial Age, a period beginning approximately 2,500 years ago, in which religion took on a new otherworldly quality, creating a place where morality could exist apart from, and in judgment of, nature (see Halton 2019). People became *separate from* nature, and could define themselves collectively as standing separate from, above, and in opposition to, it.

Fast-forwarding to the U.S., late nineteenth and early twentieth century, Progressive Era reformers such as Theodore Roosevelt began to view nature as a public good to be quantified, managed, and conserved, while Romantics such as John Muir gave rise to a distinctively U.S.-American brand of romanticism founded on the unspoiled natural world as valuable in itself, at once a spiritual retreat and a vacation spot (Berry 2015; Purdy 2015, 37–40). One source of tension—and confusion—is that the Progressive Era version of managing nature as a public good to be managed wisely and ethically was often referred to as *conservation.* However, in the context of the religion–environment connection as measured here, the story of *conservation* results in something more in line with John Muir's vision, which gave rise to a national parks system among other efforts. This "protest against nature" took a novel turn in the twentieth century, as ecology and other natural sciences upended the fixed vision of nature and replaced it with visions of flux, change, fragility, and instability, highlighting complex moral implications that are still being debated and untangled in both ecology and other scientific fields (Hamlin and Lodge 2006, 6–10). The assumption of nature as a static, wild, *thing* to be tamed gradually gave a way to a more interrelated view, in which human beings are compelled to rethink this relationship to nature with the rise of human-created global hazards. It is increasingly evident, even taken for granted, that human beings both impact the planet in profound ways and have brought into their own service the nightmarish means by which to permanently disfigure or extinguish life on earth. How these developments come to be defined as *wicked problems* is ultimately dependent on various moral currents and the narratives that underpin them. *Conservation* in the sense used here took on a view that human activity was potentially if not necessarily destructive to the integrity of the natural world, and efforts were required to preserve nature from undue human interference.

A policy-informing story beginning with the Progressive Era and carrying forward to present-day mainstream environmentalism aligns closely with the vision of *stewardship* in this work. This is a cause for confusion, given that much of the policy-informed work of the early twentieth century viewed nature as something to be wisely managed rather than set aside from human interference. *Stewardship* as an ethic implies that human beings have a responsibility to nature, even if, and in fact *because*, they exist apart from, and in tension with, it. Stewardship means a recognition that people are dependent on the environment in order to survive, even as they take for granted the necessity of transforming it for human benefit. Good stewards clean up their messes, avoid being wasteful or frivolous with resources, and view the environment as something that can be potentially improved by human activity, but the fruits of which must be sustained and protected for the benefit of future generations.

In a way, the ethical judgments of colonialism make it easier to see how First Peoples often lived in a more harmonious relationship with nature than their European counterparts. But it would be too simplistic to argue that the European colonists did not have, let alone could not attain, a stewardship ethic. Historian Mark Stoll (2015) found evidence of a stewardship ethic among the Puritans, couched in the language of their austere Protestantism. In other words, "sin" lay also in undue wastefulness and greed in one's relationship to the surrounding environment. Echoes of this can be found in environmental literature developed by Southern Baptists and other theologically conservative/culturally orthodox groups (see Land and Moore 1992). One straightforward definition of a *steward* is to be a person charged with responsibly looking after the property of another. This establishes a specific relationship between God, humans, and nature in the Christian tradition that calls for human beings to responsibly manage the earth, and nature, which ultimately belongs to God. That the environment is something that should be both *improved* and *protected* by conscientious care and effective decision-making is enshrined in the *stewardship* ethic.

Such ideas are also common in modern-day secular, policy-focused versions of environmentalism (particularly the more moderate, mainstream versions). Though these ideals were shaped by social movements that arose in the mid-twentieth century, they moved into the mainstream in the U.S. in the 1970s, but became more fragmented and polarizing, both politically and culturally, as the twentieth century drew to a close (see Mooney 2005; Oreskes and Conway 2010). Some of the reasons for this are more closely examined later in this chapter.

RELIGION AND ENVIRONMENTAL CONCERN: A BIGGER PICTURE

The theme I set forth in the first chapter—that environmental change is something that can be *witnessed*—means that *all* human communities necessarily establish a relationship with nature that can be defined, to some degree, in terms of both *stewardship* and *conservation*. This theme exists alongside a vision of *reflexivity*, which, again, is the self-reflective capacity of human beings, and the institutions they build and sustain in the face of modern hazards (see Beck 1992; Giddens 1990, 2000). In this context, religious groups, like other human institutions, have a reflexive capacity to approach environmental change, as well as other kinds of potential hazards. In addition, religion plays an important role in defining human relationships with nature, along both cosmic and moral lines. As a sociologist of religion Peter Berger (1967) once remarked, "religion is the audacious attempt to conceive of the entire universe as humanly significant" (30).

If ethics tells people what to do, then culture is the environment in which people learn how to do (or not do) it. As this work attests so far, culture can be described as a set of patterns, which interlock with, and chafe against, one another. Cultures change, and institutions change; they are *reflexive,* or *self-reflective,* but change often takes place gradually and unevenly, and the specific motivations that underpin change are often both complicated and difficult to parse. As shown in chapter 3, both culture and institutional expectations—as well as changes—are passed on to people through *habitus* via learning and socialization from an early age. This means detecting cultural change within institutions involves looking at different groups of people *born into* a specific cultural or institutional framework over a relatively long period of time.

Religion is an interesting case in point because it may have profound effects on how people come to see "the environment," but also because it is an example of an institution we are often "born into." To get an idea of whether, and how, religious institutions have responded to environmental change, I first examined religious *upbringing.* The next logical step, in understanding how religious *groups* have reflexively responded to environmental change, is measuring how change occurs among different groups of people born at roughly the same time—*birth cohorts,* or *generations.* The task of this chapter, then, is to make sense of how different religious groups have responded to both stewardship and conservation across birth cohorts, consider some reasons why these patterns hold, and visit other plausible explanations for these changes.

To restate and clarify, I developed birth cohorts based on approximately 15-year intervals. I have data going back to 1973, and the oldest person in 1973 was 89, so the oldest people in the study were born in 1884. Because this analysis was based on information as recent as 2014, and the General Social Survey only surveys adults (age 18 and older), the youngest people in the study were born in 1996. It would be an understatement to say that a lot has happened in the 112 years between the birth of the oldest and youngest persons. Also, 15-year-intervals do not necessarily capture every way in which people differed—how could they? The result, then, is best thought of as a "big picture" of environmental concern based on seven cohorts (before 1905, 1905–1919, 1920–1934, 1935–1949, 1950–1964, 1965–1979, 1980 and later) in terms of stewardship and conservation.

This is the most straightforward way to show how environmental concern has changed over this time period, but there are limitations to focusing on *cohort effects*. What if people change their minds as they get older (age effects), or when things happen around them in a given year (year effects)? That is why I have also included some models which separate age effects and year effects later in the chapter. Also, after looking at stewardship and conservation by religious groups and birth cohorts, I briefly visit some non-Judeo-Christian groups, explain why they weren't a bigger part of the study, and describe some ways to learn more about them. Then, I try to make sense of *why* things changed the way they did (or didn't) across the generations, in each religious group.

As with chapter 3, all percentages have been placed in a single table (see table 4.1). Unlike chapter 3, these are for *adults* based on their reported religious group identity, rather than based on religious upbringing. Also, unlike chapter 3, these get a bit more complicated. The reason for this has to do with the model-building process. In this case, the model "told" me that each religious group changed *differently* in terms of birth cohorts. Not only did each religious group's oldest members have different levels of environmental concern, they also changed in their levels of environmental concern at different rates from one cohort to another. The result is a table that's a bit more crowded, but also a bigger picture in which to situate and compare the differences in environmental concern by religious groups from chapter 3.

Again, the first column, %Tot, describes the "market share" of each group. Notice the slight differences in the stewardship and conservation market shares. The reason why there is a difference between stewardship and conservation is that conservation was not measured until 1984, and stewardship measures began in 1973. That means the stewardship data goes back nine years further, and contains a larger number of people. It is telling that the more recent conservation data gives a somewhat different picture of the U.S.-American religious landscape. For instance, every Protestant religious identity except for fundamentalist other Protestants (who held steady) and the Nondenominational (who grew by one percentage point) is smaller after 1984 than it was after 1973, hinting at shifts within Protestant groups during that time period. Jewish and Catholic percentages remained steady at 25 percent and 2 percent, respectively, and the *other religion* group gained one percentage point. The unaffiliated gained five percentage points of the religious landscape after 1984 relative to 1973. These percentages, together, suggest

Table 4.1   Percent Expressing Environmental Concern by Religion, Cohort

% Stewardship		Cohort							
	%Tot	0	1	2	3	4	5	6	Sig.
Baptist	20	34	44	54	61	67	70	72	***
Methodist	9	35	47	59	68	75	81	85	***
Presbyterian	4	41	49	58	64	68	71	71	n/s
Lutheran	7	31	42	53	61	67	72	74	***
Episcopalian	2	43	52	61	67	71	74	75	n/s
Nondenominational	9	34	44	53	60	65	68	70	**
Fundamentalist Prot.	2	33	40	47	52	55	56	55	**
Moderate Protestant	2	32	42	52	59	65	69	71	***
Liberal Protestant	5	42	52	62	69	74	78	80	n/s
Catholic	25	38	47	56	62	66	68	69	*
Jewish	2	56	60	64	65	64	62	58	*
Other Religion	4	42	50	59	65	69	71	71	n/s
None (Reference)	9	**47**	55	63	67	71	72	71	***

% Conservation		Cohort							
	%Tot	0	1	2	3	4	5	6	Sig.
Baptist	19	22	29	34	38	41	43	44	**
Methodist	8	21	27	31	35	37	37	37	*
Presbyterian	3	15	23	30	35	40	43	45	**
Lutheran	5	41	42	43	42	40	37	32	n/s
Episcopalian	2	35	38	40	41	41	39	37	n/s
Nondenominational	9	20	24	27	29	29	28	26	**
Fundamentalist Prot.	1	18	24	29	33	35	36	37	*
Moderate Protestant	1	39	42	43	42	41	38	35	**
Liberal Protestant	6	16	24	30	35	39	42	43	n/s
Catholic	25	23	29	33	36	37	38	37	*
Jewish	2	24	29	32	34	35	35	33	n/s
Other Religion	5	33	37	39	40	40	39	37	n/s
None (Reference)	14	**35**	39	41	43	43	42	40	**

Note: Stewardship N=34,266, Conservation N=16,687. Cohort 0=before 1905, Cohort 1=1905–1919, Cohort 2=1920–1934, Cohort 3=1935–1949, Cohort 4=1950–1964, Cohort 5=1965–1979, Cohort 6=1980–1996. Cohort^2 main effect and religion*cohort conditional effects applied to calculate model-predicted percentages. Both cohort main effects high sig. in stewardship model, and low/moderate sig. respectively in conservation model.

Controls: Attend Religious Services Weekly or More, High Confidence in Scientific Community, High Confidence in Organized Religion, Education, Sex, Race, income, Region, Size of Town/City, Political Party, Feelings about the Bible (Conservation model only).

that most Protestant groups lost ground during this time period, and that the lost ground was largely ceded to the unaffiliated (and a bit to other religions). If that sounds like support for the "secularization axiom" I criticized a bit in chapter 1, note that these are *current trends*, not projections of what will happen in the future. However, they do in fact point to a U.S. that became both more *secular* (in terms of fewer people identifying as affiliated with an established religious group) and more *multicultural* (in terms of more people identifying with groups that are not Judeo-Christian) in recent decades.

Sociologists make lousy prophets, but these trends, and the cultural anxieties connected to them, have social and political significance which is discussed further in the coming chapters.

Stewardship increased overall, across all religious identity groups, from the oldest birth cohort (0) to the youngest (6). Choose any religious group, in terms of stewardship, and cohort 6 expresses more environmental concern than cohort 0. This lines up with religion–environment research by sociologists Juliet Carlisle and April Clark (2018), who argued, based on a different analysis of the same data set, that environmental concern across religious groups grew because younger cohorts in the U.S. are more environmentally concerned than older cohorts *in general*. This is true, but the way I measured religious groups here reveals some important differences across religious groups. Younger cohorts are generally more environmentally concerned than older cohorts, but different groups "started" at different levels, and environmental concern began to "flatten out," or grow more slowly, among the more recent cohorts (4 through 6). I offer some reasons why later in this chapter.

Lowest levels of stewardship in the oldest cohort (0) were found among Lutherans, as well as fundamentalist and moderate other Protestants, followed closely by Baptists and the Nondenominational. Highest levels were found among Jewish persons, followed by the unaffiliated. Lutherans are typically considered more culturally and theologically moderate, whereas Baptists are predominantly culturally and theologically fundamentalist (this is reflected in how they are categorized in the General Social Survey; see Smith 1990). On the other hand, every religious group except Jewish persons expressed stewardship at lower levels than the religiously unaffiliated in the oldest cohort. By the most recent cohort (6), things look rather different. Methodists and liberal Protestants express the highest levels of stewardship, and most religious groups (with the notable exception of fundamentalist Protestants and Jewish persons) roughly match or outpace the unaffiliated. Presbyterians, Episcopalians, liberal Protestants, and other religious groups are not significantly different from the unaffiliated in terms of stewardship overall (n/s). All other groups are significantly different in that levels of stewardship grew *faster* among religious groups than among the unaffiliated (with the exception of Jewish persons, for whom the trend was more "bell-shaped," and highest levels of stewardship were found among Jewish persons born into roughly the "baby boomer" generation). *Religious groups, almost without exception, grew faster in levels of stewardship than the unaffiliated, catching up to (and in some cases surpassing) them by the most recent cohort.* On average, millennials (cohort 6) who identify as Baptist, Methodist, Lutheran, Episcopalian, and liberal Protestant are *more* environmentally concerned in terms of stewardship than the unaffiliated.

In terms of conservation, however, Lutherans in the oldest cohort (0) held the highest levels, followed by liberal Protestants, then Episcopalians and the unaffiliated. Lowest levels are found among Presbyterians, as well as fundamentalist and moderate other Protestants, and the Nondenominational. In the most recent cohort (6), Lutherans are nearer the lower levels of conservation, having actually *decreased*, as have moderate Protestants. Here, Baptists, Presbyterians, and the Nondenominational hold the highest levels of conservation, outpacing even the unaffiliated. Lutherans, Episcopalians, the Nondenominational, Jewish persons, and other religious groups are not significantly different from the unaffiliated in terms of conservation overall (n/s). But again, *religious groups, almost without exception, grew faster in levels of conservation than the unaffiliated, catching up to (and in some cases surpassing) them.*

Competing Explanations

In other words, religious groups grew faster, and were more dynamic, than the unaffiliated across cohorts in terms of environmental concern across both measures. In general, this was religious groups "catching up" to the unaffiliated, but there were also a few religious groups that expressed *higher* levels of environmental concern on one or both measures, particularly in cohort 6 (those born in 1980 or later). At least two questions arise: first, how do these shifts fit into the context of the religious motives discussed in the previous chapters? And second, how do these shifts fit into broader historical dimensions of religious and cultural change in the U.S.?

First, I'll compare these results to the results from chapter 3. Note the differences, percentage wise, in terms of expected results. Results ranged in the 30s and 40s for stewardship and the 20s and 30s for conservation, percentage wise, in chapter 3, but they ranged as high as the 80s for stewardship and into the 40s for conservation in table 4.1. This is because chapter 3 results were an *average* across *all* birth cohorts, and these are *changes across* birth cohorts. This also points to fairly consistent upward trends toward higher levels of environmental concern overall, especially in terms of stewardship. Also, based on chapter 3, the unaffiliated are really two distinct groups in terms of environmental concern—those who are unaffiliated and were raised that way (a minority, who hold fairly similar levels of environmental concern to religious groups) and those who were raised religious and disaffiliated later in life (a majority, who hold the highest levels of environmental concern on average). Basically, given this catching up and some surpassing when comparing religious groups to the unaffiliated (who are mostly ex-religious people), many religious groups have likely had some positive effect on environmental concern. But which groups, and why?

According to chapter 3, the groups with the highest levels of stewardship in terms of upbringing were Jewish persons, liberal Protestants, Episcopalians, and Presbyterians—all groups that outpaced the unaffiliated. Only Jewish persons outpaced the unaffiliated in cohort 0, but many groups, including Baptists, Methodists, Lutherans, Episcopalians, and liberal Protestants, held higher levels of stewardship than the unaffiliated in cohort 6. In other words, on average, being born into a more theologically liberal group is linked to higher levels of environmental concern (chapter 3), but younger Christians *in general* are more environmentally concerned. This effect isn't as strong when comparing younger Christians to the generations directly before them—cohorts 4 and 5 are not that different from cohort 6, but most have still increased a bit. It was really between those born before 1950 and those born after—between those born roughly into the "greatest generation" and the "baby boomers"—where the biggest changes happened.

Returning to the chapter 3 upbringing results in terms of conservation, most groups held similar levels to those raised unaffiliated—with *higher* levels among those raised Baptist and those raised Episcopalian. In able 4.1, the unaffiliated outpaced every group except Lutherans and Episcopalians in cohort 0, but Presbyterians, Baptists, and the Nondenominational had higher levels of conservation in cohort 6 than the unaffiliated. Once again, cohort 6 overall has the highest levels of conservation, but the greatest changes occurred between those born before 1950 and those born after.

Now, returning to the types of religious motives, and drawing on some of the original research, I can add some important details. Both attending religious services at least once a week and having high confidence in organized religion are significantly *negatively* related to stewardship. This, again, calls Type 1, or *direct*, motives into question; people are probably not expressing higher levels of environmental concern *explicitly because* they see their commitments in strictly religious terms. In addition, high confidence in the scientific community, being more highly educated, living in a more densely populated area, living in the Northeastern U.S., and identifying as or leaning Democrat are positively linked to stewardship, and were all highly statistically significant (for full regression models, see Szrot 2019, 59). This describes, on average, a certain "kind" of person who matches the Buttel (1979) model of environmental concern. In other words, people who are younger, more highly educated, more scientifically minded, urban, and politically liberal are more likely to express stewardship, independently of their religious associations. It seems more likely that connections within religious groups reflect an indirect (Type 2) motive.

This story doesn't hold up for conservation, though. Neither confidence in science nor organized religion nor being a Democrat seems to matter (though there is still a negative relationship between attending religious services weekly or more), and education is actually *negatively* linked. Whereas women were slightly more likely to express stewardship, men were more likely to express conservation, and persons of color also expressed conservation more often than whites. Bible belief had little effect, and Biblical literalists were actually slightly *more* likely than nonliteralists (but less likely than non-Bible believers) to express conservation after accounting for differences between religious groups over time. Midwesterners and rural residents had lower levels of conservation, but culturally conservative southerners and urbane, cosmopolitan northeasterners did not differ (for full model, see Szrot 2019, 63). Putting these findings together, the story for stewardship does not quite hold true for conservation, but there is a notable place for religion in both. The differences in conservation are not as consistently explained by a Type 2 motive. The question, then, is how to best capture that notable place for religion, and its role in motivating environmental concern. This question can be answered more definitely after visiting the ways that religion and culture have changed in the U.S. in recent decades.

Managing Expectations

There are a few different ways to approach the *expectations* here. That is, what are some possible ways to account for these changes, against the background of cultural and religious change? One approach would take for granted something like the "culture wars" thesis (see Hunter 1991)—that around the end of the 1960s, religious groups began to reorganize themselves around two disparate cultural identities that have increasingly drifted away from common ground. This led to splintering of historical denominations, and in part explains the tendency in sociology of religion to divide religious groups based on closeness to *fundamentalism* or literal interpretations of religious tradition (Smith 1990), or to divide Protestants into *evangelical* (more culturally and theologically conservative) and *mainline* (more culturally/ theologically moderate-to-liberal, see Steensland et al. 2000). A related idea comes out of the work of Wade Clark Roof and William McKinney (1992), that religion in the U.S. has become more of a "voluntary identity" rather than something that is *ascribed* or decided at birth. This leads U.S.-Americans, to varying degrees, to "pick and choose" religious identities (and the aspects to follow or ignore) based on ideological slants and cultural identity.

These divisions are more or less taken for granted in the social scientific study of religion, and something like this has undoubtedly happened over the past half-century. These cultural rifts are deep, and may have grown deeper of late, but the results across birth cohorts tell a more complicated story. First, each younger cohort is more environmentally concerned than the older *in general*, but these changes reach a peak and begin to flatten among those born between 1950 and 1964. These birth years overlap significantly with the "baby boomer" generation, at once steeped in radical optimism, fragmented by war, fighting to expand human rights, and now criticized (incidentally by "millennials" who overlap with the youngest cohort, 1980–1996) for taking a seemingly reactionary turn.

However, environmental concern is not unanimous in expression or uniform in its growth—this is a "big picture" based on average differences, and changes in groups over time. The gap between the highest and lowest levels of stewardship grew by five percentage points between the oldest and the youngest cohorts, but actually closed by almost ten percentage points in terms of conservation. In both, fundamentalist Protestants fell behind other religious groups, but still exhibited notable growth intergenerationally. This cannot be merely a matter of "cultural fundamentalism" (see Eve and Harrold 1990), because the largely theologically fundamentalist Baptists surpassed the unaffiliated on both measures among the youngest cohort. Environmental concern across generations does not map neatly onto existing models of religious and cultural change as *polarization,* though such models might help to explain why there is little difference between the unaffiliated and more theologically liberal Protestant religious groups. Again, cultural progressivism and stewardship seem to go together, but beyond that, this story doesn't hold especially well. Perhaps it's time to tell a somewhat different story. A third possibility is, simply, that the groups whose levels of environmental concern were most dynamic were the groups that have some historically connection to, or investment in, environmental issues. Before looking more closely at this possibility, I want to visit some of the other differences in environmental concern between religious groups.

Limitations of Big Pictures

I presented some of this work, and variations of it, several times over the past few years while working on it. It's pretty standard for scholars to do this—talking about work in progress helps with figuring out what to focus on, what to clarify, and what questions to anticipate. One question I got a lot involves the categories I've used. In particular, they're mostly focused on Christianity—this, people have noted, makes it seem like I'm not interested in religion and the environment so much as *Christianity* and the environment. My short response is that, from this "big-picture" view, there just aren't enough members of many groups to actually analyze change over time. This is a long-standing problem when doing this kind of big-picture research—the fine-grained detail gets lost. It's a bit like zooming out in a photograph or image. Even in a really good image, little details blur and disappear, leaving the broad contours. Extending the metaphor, taking a picture "from afar" or "from above" and then zooming in makes the details grainy and inaccurate. I don't want to do grainy, inaccurate analysis, making big claims based on little data, but I don't want to ignore details either, so this is a compromise, as well as a way to illuminate how the dynamics above can be explained.

Based on figure 4.1, the highest levels of stewardship are found among Native Americans, Buddhists, and other eastern religions. These are followed by the unaffiliated, Muslims, Hindus, interdenominational persons, and other Christians. Highest levels of conservation are found among Muslims and other eastern religions, and lowest levels are among Orthodox Christians and Native Americans. Both Catholics and Protestants, when viewed as groups in a "snapshot," are very similar to the average levels of environmental concern for the U.S. (all groups), and are lower in environmental concern than most other religious groups, including the unaffiliated. This snapshot, including all persons and not accounting for differences in upbringing or change over time, can be illuminating in its limitations. It illustrates some meaningful differences between groups that have been passed over in relative silence so far, but also shows how groups like Protestants are quite different when subdividing and examining them more closely.

In many cases, these cannot be considered *representative samples* of the total population of these groups, because the number of people who are actually part of the data set is not large enough. For example, I cannot reasonably base a view of all Native Americans in the U.S. on twenty-three people in this sample. Even in groups for which I have somewhat larger samples, like Muslims, there are so few in some years that I can't say anything meaningful about how Muslims in the U.S. have changed over time in levels of environmental concern. Though there are more Muslims in the U.S. now as a market share of religion than there were in the past, Muslims are still around 1 percent of the U.S. population, and were significantly smaller in terms of market share decades ago.

The other side of this problem could extend to the religious groups themselves. For example, "Baptist" is actually an umbrella category containing a lot of diversity—there are lots of different groups of Baptists in the U.S. How different from one another might they be, and in how many ways? These are interesting questions; subdividing these groups further would mean not enough people in each group to make meaningful comparisons across long periods of time (and I would also run up against the limits of available categories in the survey data based on when and how questions were asked). As the story arc so far has hopefully made clear, it's important to focus on *long-term trends* when trying to understand the religion–environment connection. In my view, focusing on long-term trends is useful more broadly in the social sciences, but it's especially helpful when studying cultural or ethical change,

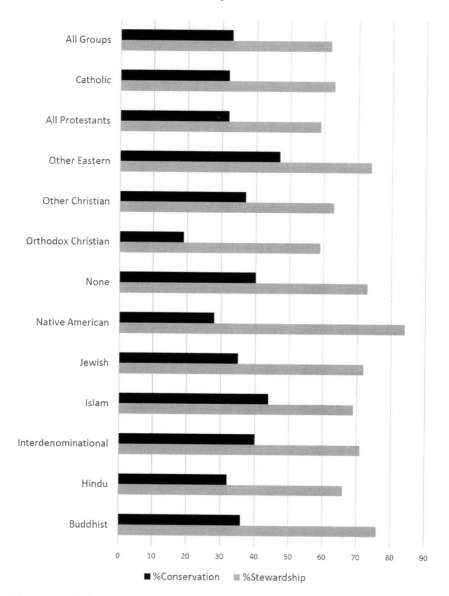

Figure 4.1 Environmental Concern by Religious Affiliation.

or institutional responses to something as complex, multifaceted—*wicked*— as environmental change.

Because of their small size, I cannot systematically analyze these groups, and so these results are not based on having "controlled for" anything. For example, a Buddhist who recently relocated from Cambodia to a small town in the Midwest is going to be culturally different from a Buddhist convert born in suburban California and raised Protestant. In fact, this is one of the other limitations to studying adult religious belief as related to birth cohort. It is clear from chapter 3 that disaffiliation meaningfully affects environmental concern. It is less clear how *conversion* would affect environmental concern, or even whether environmental concern could itself drive conversion, especially given how many different ways conversion could occur.

Any effort to compare these results is speculation, and I'm hesitant to speculate too much based on the limited evidence here. Maybe Native Americans have the highest stewardship and the lowest conservation because of historical dimensions noted in the beginning of this chapter—stewardship may have deep cultural roots among First Peoples, but conservation has a grim history of being used as a racist project to displace First Peoples from their land by defining those lands as improperly used or even "uninhabited" (see Purdy 2015; Sawyer 2004, 55). Maybe the relationship between Islam and higher levels of environmental concern is indirect, due to the demographic composition of Muslim immigrants—particularly, being more likely urban and middle class, and avoiding affiliation with the U.S. Republican Party given its "chilly" reception to Muslims in general (see Pew Research Center 2014). It is also possible that the desire to be "good neighbors" (including becoming "greener") arose partly as an effort to combat negative stereotypes and cultural hostilities after events such as September 11, 2001. There is evidence from field research that this might be the case (see Baugh 2017, 144–6). Of course, some religions might have an easier time incorporating environmental concern into their cultural frameworks than others, but taking this possibility seriously would involve extensive interpretive work in philosophy and comparative religion, as well as field research—which is beyond the scope of this story. In any case, I would need to know more in order to show whether or not my speculations have weight. This is normal in science—admitting ignorance and a willingness to learn more in the future is part of the process.

However, what these small-scale speculations point to is a way of addressing, and more importantly *simplifying,* the findings from the past two chapters by drawing on a broader historical context. That is, my upcoming "third explanation" compares historical developments within both religious groups and environmentalism to these statistical trends. The biggest changes in stewardship and conservation happened in terms of birth cohorts in those born between 1950 and 1964, cohort 4, or the so-called "baby boomers." Also, changes continued upward in the most recent cohorts, 5 and 6 (roughly "generation X" and the "millennials"), but they happened more slowly. This means asking two more questions. *First, what drove this apparent "slowdown" in more recent generations? Second, what happened in the early-to-mid-twentieth century that drove these upward trends in environmental concern in religious groups?*

YEAR, AGE, AND THEOLOGY:
COMPARING APPROACHES

As noted in chapter 2, *cohort effects* assume that there's something relatively stable about the years in which people are born that influence the results. It's assumed that people are born into religion, for the most part, and that by looking at *when* people are born, as related to a religious group, makes it possible to detect the influence of religion on environmental concern. If there is something wrong with this assumption, then it would influence any historical explanation that could be offered in terms of the changes described in this chapter. Therefore, it makes sense to look at the possibility of *year effects* (whether environmental concern changes based on "current events") as well as *age effects* (whether environmental concern changes as people get older) before concluding.

Again, statistical models of the social world are best thought of as "useful simplifications" of what is happening, and what has happened. Think about it: how many variables are there in the social world, potentially? Every model has to select certain things to focus on, because of the vast, potentially infinite, number of possible things that could influence an outcome like environmental concern. When it comes to sociology, both ethics and logistics mean it's often just not possible to set up controlled experiments in laboratories. In such cases, studying a problem from several different angles to see how models agree, or disagree, with one another is the best bet. The goal is for a kind of *consilience,* or "jumping off together," where several lines of evidence based on different assumptions point in the same direction, even if each of those lines of evidence is far from perfect on its own (see Gould 2011; Shermer 2003, 144; Wilson 1998).

Having said that, I developed several models that were based on very different assumptions from the last set. In particular, I wanted to see whether or not a picture that focused on *year effects, age effects,* and theological orientation added to, complicated, or explained away the "big picture" unfolding so far. Being that what I have described so far complicates and challenges some established explanations of the religion–environment connection, I also wanted to carefully account for the role of age and cultural/theological differences, because these have been central aspects of the research on environmental concern in environmental sociology and sociology of religion, respectively. This kind of model is a lot more complicated than a cohort model, and I won't revisit the gory details here (for more information, revisit the second half of chapter 2, and/or see Szrot 2019). Basically, it involves parsing the year effects, group effects, and age effects so that they can be analyzed separately from one another. Each can be thought of as existing on a different level of the model. This way,

Table 4.2 Stewardship and Conservation by Year, Theology, and Age

%Stewardship	Fundamentalist			Moderate			Liberal		
Year	25yo	45yo	65yo	25yo	45yo	65yo	25yo	45yo	65yo
1973	40	25	14	42	26	14	45	30	19
1974	43	27	15	44	28	16	47	33	21
1975	45	29	17	47	30	17	50	35	2
1976	48	31	18	49	32	18	52	37	24
1977	50	33	20	52	34	20	55	39	26
1978	53	35	21	54	36	22	57	42	28
1980	57	40	25	59	41	25	62	47	32
1982	62	45	29	64	46	29	67	52	36
1983	64	47	31	66	48	31	69	54	39
1984	67	50	33	68	51	33	71	57	41
1985	69	52	35	70	53	36	73	59	44
1986	71	55	38	72	56	38	75	61	46
1987	73	57	40	74	58	40	76	64	48
1988	75	60	42	76	61	43	78	66	51
1989	77	62	45	78	63	45	80	68	53
1990	78	64	47	80	65	48	81	70	56
1991	**80**	**67**	**50**	**81**	**67**	**50**	**83**	**72**	**58**
1993	78	65	49	79	66	49	81	71	58
1994	77	64	49	78	65	49	80	70	57
1996	74	62	48	75	63	48	78	68	57
1998	71	60	47	73	61	48	75	66	56
2000	68	58	46	70	59	47	73	64	55
2002	65	56	46	67	57	46	70	62	54
2004	62	54	45	64	55	45	67	60	54
2006	59	52	44	61	53	45	64	58	53
2008	56	50	44	57	51	44	60	56	52
2010	52	48	43	54	49	43	57	54	52
2012	49	46	42	51	47	43	54	52	51
2014	46	44	42	47	45	42	50	50	50
Conservation (%, all years)	**38**	**32**	**26**	**36**	**30**	**25**	**39**	**33**	**27**

Note: General Social Survey data not available for 1979, 1981, 1992, all odd-numbered years after 1994. Models accounted for gaps in year variable, but data for these years inferred based on existing data.

Controls: Attend Religious Services Weekly or More, High Confidence in Scientific Community, High Confidence in Organized Religion, Education, Sex, Race, income, Region, Size of Town/City, Political Party, Feelings about the Bible (Conservation model only).

it becomes possible to describe the relationship between age and cultural/ theological differences over time.

Table 4.2 contains the results of these efforts. For stewardship, there is a year-by-year difference, and for conservation, there is not. That is because when the models were first estimated, it turned out that conservation *fluctuated* a little bit, year by year, but did not seem to go up or down significantly in a consistent pattern. In other words, the *year effects* for conservation aren't statistically meaningful, and I can focus on the age effects (in this model) and compare them to the cohort results in others. I have not reported statistical significance in this table—that's because when you create a model like this one, you have to be careful to only include effects that matter to begin with (otherwise the model gets really big and really messy really fast), and to make sure that the way that changes, year by year, are captured makes sense both logically and in terms of how the model is built. In other words, *age matters when it comes to conservation, but both year and age matter when it comes to stewardship.*

So, what happened in 1992? In 1992, the Rio de Janeiro Earth Summit was intended to be a global effort to engage with, and "get ahead of," the potential dangers of climate change driven by human activity (Oreskes and Conway 2010, 197; Vidal 2012). A strong and consistent U.S. partisan pushback followed the conference, as critics viewed the regulations necessary to combat dangerous climate change as corruption of the principles of free enterprise and evidence of creeping socialism (Oreskes and Conway 2010, 197–215, 247–51). This launched a decades-long (and ongoing) effort to sow doubt about the role human beings are playing in changing the earth's climate. The 1990s also saw the escalation of the "culture wars"—a growing rift between *cultural progressivism* and *cultural orthodoxy* around which the Democratic and Republican parties organized (see Chaves 2017; Hunter 1991). The struggles that emerged in this time period are still noticeable (and likely even stronger) in the U.S. today—as I write this, 28 years later, there is ongoing ideological tension surrounding the content and use of the word *socialism,* cultural battles surrounding the role of religion in public decision-making, and implications on both sides of the political aisle for future environmental concern, policy, and global governance. As a "turning point" in environmental attitudes and policy, it would be difficult to find a more significant historical moment than 1992.

This also makes for a great opportunity to test whether, and how, religion and cohort effects stand up alongside age, year, and theological effects. I basically divided the entire data set in half at 1992 to see what kinds of tendencies would arise. What I found was rather surprising. First, note that the age gap for stewardship was rather large in 1973—fully 26 percentage points between 25-year-old and 65-year-old fundamentalists, and the same gap among liberals (though liberals were more likely to express stewardship than fundamentalists, overall). The "age gap" actually widened a bit by 1991, with 30 points among fundamentalists and 31 points among moderates, but a slight narrowing—25 points—among liberals. Note, again, that these are theological orientations, and can serve as "stand-ins" for cultural orientations, but they aren't the same thing as political ideologies. After 1991, both theological orientation and age slowly become less important—the gap actually *closes.*

By 2014, liberals don't differ by age anymore, moderates by only five points, and fundamentalists, by only four. That probably seems counterintuitive. Even though there is a reversal in the trends after 1992, and the model captures that *effects of religion in general*, at least as measured liberal-moderate-fundamentalist, declined. Put another way, stewardship declines after 1992 *for reasons other than age or theological orientation.* There are still changes by year, but they are gradual (for full model and estimation procedures, see Szrot 2019, 107–16).

Before putting this into the "bigger picture" developed in the first half of this chapter, the conservation numbers are worth visiting briefly. As I noted above, there aren't significant "year effects" for conservation, but there are differences by theological orientation and age. The highest levels of conservation overall are found among liberals, but fundamentalists are close in conservation levels, and moderates hold the lowest levels. They are all within a few percentage points of one another, and do reflect a decline across all groups with age. In other words, theological orientation in general doesn't affect conservation in some even and clear way. That is, defining people as "fundamentalist," "moderate," and "liberal" doesn't predict levels of conservation very well. Age, on the other hand, does—younger people overall are notably more likely to express conservation than older people. To sum up, year doesn't much matter with conservation, and neither does theology—but age *does* (for full model and estimation procedures, see Szrot 2019, 116–9).

So, how does looking at theology, year, and age in these multilevel models change the "big picture" when compared to the cohort analysis? If cultural divides were driving people apart on environmental issues, then these divides would show up in both stewardship and conservation, and they would mean that fundamentalists and liberals would grow further apart over the course of the last 25 years or so. Such changes didn't show up with conservation, and actually pointed to the other direction with stewardship. There *is* cultural polarization, and there *are* culture wars, but people are on average *less* divided year by year on environmental issues as measured here *in terms of culture.* The distinction between "fundamentalists" who don't express environmental concern and "liberals" who do is a rather small part of a bigger picture, involving how things have changed over time. This invites, once more, a "third explanation": to understand the history of religion and environmental concern, different measures of religion help to parse out the groups that are more, or less, likely to be environmentally concerned.

When it comes to age and stewardship, the "age gap" actually increased through 1991, and then began to decrease afterward. Clearly age matters, at least filtered through the prism of theology. However, age becomes less important beginning in 1993. Age also matters when it comes to conservation, mostly independently of year or theology. The environmental sociologists, and the Buttel model of environmental concern (1979), continue to make an interesting contribution (age matters), but the contribution of age is lessened by "bringing religion in."

For now, I can say at least three things about this set of year, age, theology models: first, differences in environmental concern by religion cannot be neatly reduced to recent cultural/theological divides (theology and/or year effects). Second, year matters, such that theology matters less after 1993, meaning something other than year and theology is driving these changes. Third, age matters, but it "matters less" after 1993 as well, at least when it comes to stewardship. In other words, religion plays a varied but dynamic role in predicting environmental concern, but its effects begin to level off more recently. This generally agrees with the birth cohort models from earlier in the chapter, and also suggests that dividing religious groups in more fine-grained terms reveals novel dynamics specific to religion that cannot be explained away by cultural or political polarization.

CHAPTER SUMMARY: TOWARD A THIRD EXPLANATION

The statistical work from this chapter, showing an uptick in environmental concern that is especially marked among multiple religious groups, accords with documented historical trends. To pick up with the historical narratives from the beginning of this chapter, especially the work of historian Mark Stoll (2015), "Many things fall neatly into place when the historical trajectory of U.S.-American environmentalism is regarded as a sort of para-religious movement or an expression of Reformed Protestant belief and culture" (267). This "Reformed Protestant cultural expression" manifested itself among the Puritans during the colonial period, but found fuller expression during the Progressive Era movements in the late nineteenth and early twentieth century. I noted in chapter 3, based on Stoll's (2015) work, how the efforts toward enshrining both stewardship and conservation as policy were spearheaded by Presbyterian elites, carried forward by secularizing Protestant scientific and cultural voices. It is interesting, then, that the oldest cohort Presbyterians in this chapter were the *least* likely to express conservation, and held only middling levels of stewardship (see table 4.1). However, Presbyterians expressed the *highest* levels of conservation in the youngest cohorts, notably higher than the religiously unaffiliated as well as most other groups, and did not differ significantly from the unaffiliated in levels of stewardship. Presbyterian political elites, such as those involved in the Progressive Era reforms, gave rise to various environmental protections as well as protected wilderness (Stoll 2015). Later, scientific and cultural voices ranging from Rachel Carson to John Denver operated as "social carriers" (see Weber 2011, 48–9) to carry the ethical and cultural basis of those policy decisions forward in time, but it took generations to manifest in the general public as higher levels of conservation ethic. Again, the United Presbyterian Church became the first U.S.-American religious denomination to officially enshrine environmental issues into doctrine, in 1971 (see Yaple 1982).

Some of the earliest evidence of a Catholic turn toward environmental concern emerges at approximately the same time, with Paul VI bringing Catholic social teaching to bear on themes of overconsumption, and challenging the moral basis of technological and economic domination (see, for example, Raven 2016; Szrot 2020a). Catholics, however, have expressed middling levels of environmental concern overall. If the "social carriers" thesis is correct, then a future of widespread Catholic environmentalism will manifest itself in coming decades, and this story is just too early to demonstrate what these developments will look like. Databases such as the collection of faith statements on the environment by the *Earth Ministry,* as well as the work conducted around the themes of religion and ecology at the Yale Divinity School, have current purchase on the religion–environment connection (for an extensive online list of religious engagement with ecological issues, see Grim and Tucker 2014, 208–10). These show that between the early 1970s and the early 1990s, religious groups with differing theological commitments, who staked out very different positions in the coming "culture wars," responded constructively to environmental concern and made environmental concern part of their faith, with official statements of faith, books, educational pamphlets, and other efforts. In particular, there are familiar denominations within Baptist, Methodist, Presbyterian, Lutheran, Episcopalian, Catholic, and many other religious groups that have expressed officially a commitment to environmental concern. The growth in environmental concern across birth cohorts here is best thought of as long-term responses, shaped the kinds of commitments expressed, as well as how they fit within the broader cultural framework of the religious group and its membership.

However, this raises some interesting questions in terms of *causality,* which is the bigger idea underpinning the range of religious motives discussed so far. That is, if environmental concern had already been mostly cultivated among the general public by cohort 4 (those born between 1950 and 1964), and if an environmental ethic, in religious terms, is part of a *habitus* learned in early life, then what bearing could these developments have on developing this ethic? The increase in environmental concern across birth cohorts had mostly happened years *before* the wide-ranging moves toward including environmental concern in official religious doctrine. Baby boomers were adults, and many were already parents themselves, by the time religious groups really began making environmental concern part of doctrine in a wide-spread and consistent manner.

History offers some hints as to which way the causal arrow points, as well as what kinds of religious motivation are taking place. For instance, Rachel Carson's watershed work on environmentalism *Silent Spring* was published in 1962 (see Carson 2002 [1962]), fully nine years before environmental concern became an official part of the Presbyterian faith. In addition, the keystone text in the religion–environment connection, Lynn White Jr.'s (1967) *The Historical Roots of Our Ecological Crisis,* called for St. Francis of Assisi as a guide to a greener Christianity in 1967. The Catholic Church under John Paul II (1979) issued a papal bull making Francis of Assisi the patron saint of ecology in 1979, fully 12 years later. In fact, the year before Carson's work debuted, the Catholic Church under John XXIII made explicit its commitment to human dominion over nature in the papal Encyclical letter *Mater et Magistra* (1961):

> Besides, the resources which God in His goodness and wisdom has implanted in Nature are well-nigh inexhaustible, and He has at the same time given man the intelligence to discover ways and means of exploiting these resources for his own advantage and his own livelihood. The real solution of the problem is not to be found in expedients which offend against the divinely established moral order and which attack human life at its very source, but in a renewed scientific and technical effort no man's part to deepen and extend his dominion over Nature (189).

Putting together this selection of influential historical events and linking it to statistical trends, the simplest explanation is that present-day environmentalism, the environmentalism of the 1960s, of Rachel Carson and of latter-day social movements, was not born in the churches, but originated in the broader culture and was internalized by the churches later. Consistently high levels of stewardship and conservation *follow* the baby boomer generation because those ideas made their way into religious groups via these cultural carriers, and becoming part of official doctrine made it more likely that they would be carried forward through childhood socialization of later generations. Environmental concern and commitment, at a deeper and more enduring ethical level, is most effectively cultivated in early childhood as part of a cultural *habitus.* Both families and religion are uniquely positioned to do so.

However, stopping here would be ignoring the rich body of historical research which connects modern ideas about the environment to multiple cultural currents dating back to centuries and woven throughout multiple religious denominations. What the "bigger picture" suggests is that concern for the environment emerged not only from scientific rationality and a growing body of evidence raising alarms about environmental change, but that such efforts were themselves shaped by an older, quasi-religious ethic rooted in understandings of the role humans play *vis a vis* nature and the divine.

This means that religious institutions, like other institutions, are *responding to* environmental change in ways that exist both *within* and *outside* those institutions. This explanation further supports the *indirect* (Type 2) and *invisible* (Type 3) motives rather than a direct cause-and-effect relationship. That is, religious groups have mobilized around shared cultural resources and social networks to respond to environmental change as detected by scientists and increasingly taken on as part of a broader cultural concern. In one sense, religious groups are taking on cultural ideas from outside; in another sense, those cultural ideas are returning to their respective sources via new generations of cultural carriers and flowering anew. What this indicates most clearly is a *capacity* for reflexivity. It is surely not an accident that highest levels of environmental concern, in both political parties, are in 1991—when a larger number of major religious groups in the U.S. had already gone on record as speaking more, and more often, about environmental issues.

What makes religious organizations, and approaches, different from other organizations and approaches is the possibility of carrying forward the social currents across generations, including ethical commitments and cultural resources devoted to addressing environmental issues long term. These may remain with those who move to a different religious group or leave organized religion later in life—such is the power of the human interactions and the connections, direct and indirect, that shape a person's life from birth. This leaves a place for an *invisible* (Type 3) motive to remain relevant, in that *highest* levels of environmental concern are found among those who leave organized religion altogether sometime after age 16. These secularized social carriers, coming of age in an era characterized by environmental changes utterly unprecedented in the history of the human species, may be uniquely positioned to make long-term cultural and ethical contributions to addressing the consequences of these environmental changes.

The religion–environment connection can be explained in terms of the history of religious groups' engagement with environmental issues and themes, but based on the historical and statistical evidence, it is not specifically *driven by* religious groups themselves. Instead, it is manifested in and perpetuated by religious groups based on broader cultural currents and responses to environmental change. This third explanation represents a sort of *institutionalized green reflexivity*, though I suspect I am not the only person to ever use this phrase. *Reflexivity,* once again, is the capacity to be self-reflective, to assess one's own position in relation to a changing environment. It is something that people, institutions, and any living thing are capable of doing—and in fact *must do in order to survive.* In this case, that *changing environment* is both the cultural environment which religious groups inhabit and the earth on which those human cultures, as well as the rest of "the environment," coexist. *Institutionalized* reflexivity at the level of religious *groups*, rather than individual people, is cultivated through those groups' responses to environmental change over decades. This kind of reflexivity can be detected—if indirectly—through changes in levels of environmental concern across birth cohorts, because religion is typically something people are "born into," learning and internalizing as part of a collection of habits of thinking and behaving from the first years of life. In this way, *institutionalized reflexivity* as institutional responses to change comes to individual people through a *habitus* (see chapter 3).

An *institutionalized green reflexivity,* then, is simply the self-reflectiveness of institutions regarding environmental change, expressed in turn by people who become cultural carriers, often without being consciously aware of it. Chapter 3 revealed clear differences in environmental concern across religious groups, but the highest levels of environmental concern were found among the *Ex's* who were raised religious but left organized religion later in life. This chapter built on those findings, revealing that religious groups in general, some more than others, have been quite dynamic in cultivating environmental concern across several generations. These dynamics cannot be explained away by age differences, changes year by year, or cultural polarization. Searching for a "third way" to explain these results means explaining how (1) a reflexive response to environmental change makes its way indirectly to members of religious groups (2) that can also be *directly located* within changes in environmental attitudes in religious groups' doctrines. In other words, these changes in environmental concern are both cultural responses to environmental change and indicators of the way religious institutions have gradually come to terms with the reality of this change.

The impacts, and predictors, of environmental concern from the perspective of religious groups take decades to manifest. *Environmental concern* arises out of a broader cultural context which shapes institutions and draws on existing cultural resources (see Polletta 2008). The personal, experiential dimension of religion also plays a role in fostering these developments. When studying faith-based environmental movements and organizations, personal events and biographies led religious persons to frame environmental issues within a faith-based perspective (Ellingson 2016, 29–53). Rather than simple "cause and effect," whereby religious groups tell members that environmental concern is a sacred moral duty, and they respond, religious groups are *embedded* in a broader cultural context in which these responses play out. What I am calling *institutionalized green reflexivity* here is the messy, multifaceted process of persons interacting with, and within, institutions in a changing cultural and environmental landscape. It is a sociological truism that people change institutions, but institutions also change people.

At least one other task remains: to more explicitly connect these trends and findings to those broader cultural currents in order to examine more closely what drives, and is driven by, religious groups' responses to environmental change. That is, the changes across generations that are described here did not occur in a vacuum—in fact, quite the opposite. The U.S. has witnessed unprecedented cultural change since the 1960s. In the span of a single lifetime for some, the cultural landscape may have been rendered unintelligible. At least three arenas of cultural change come to mind: the increased empowerment of women via women's movements and feminism, debates over economic issues and economic restructuring, and issues related to race and Civil Rights. Issues related to race are intimately connected to both the history of religious groups and political party platforms in past decades, such that a separation of race, politics, and religion would be a false one. Thus, the next chapter focuses on these issues: *how have women and men responded differently to the religion–environment connection? How have low-, middle-, and high-income persons responded differently to the religion–environment connection? How have Blacks and whites, Republicans and Democrats, responded differently to the religion–environment connection?* With some answers to these questions, I can proceed to solidify, complicate, or challenge this explanation and vision, testing whether and to what extent this institutionalized green reflexivity emerges unscathed.

Chapter 5

Bringing Religion in

Gender, Class, Race, and Politics

As with any institution, religious people shape, and are shaped by, religious institutions. Chapter 3 showed how religious upbringing, as well as disaffiliation, shaped levels of environmental concern. Chapter 4 showed how religious *groups* have changed over time in their levels of environmental concern, as a function of when members were born, as well as by year and by age. It would be possible to stop there, to wrap up the story to be told, but it seems like such a story would be incomplete, for at least three related reasons. The first is that I am a sociologist, and my discipline, at least as it has realized itself within the U.S. over the past several decades, is keenly interested in group-level differences and inequities. In particular, conversations surrounding gender, social class, and race have drawn a great deal of scrutiny in sociology; these facets of identity profoundly shape the courses of human lives. How do gender, social class, and race have shaped the religion–environment connection, past and present? To answer this question, I divide up the people in my data as described below and then "bring religion in."

The second reason has to do with the explanations I have offered over the course of the last two chapters. Chapter 3 showed why the relationship between environmental concern and religion is best thought of as indirect, even invisible. People raised in certain religious groups develop higher, or lower, levels of environmental concern. However, disaffiliation, or becoming religiously unaffiliated in later adolescence or adulthood, was linked to even higher levels of environmental concern. Additionally, *indirect* (Type 2) motives kept appearing, based on differences in levels of environmental concern *overall* by gender, income, race, and political party. These differences extended to the religiously unaffiliated as well as the religious, even when and where the unaffiliated were not that different from one another overall in terms of religious beliefs and practices and environmental concern. Building on this, chapter 4 showed that environmental concern across both measures did not neatly reduce to a binary division between "cultural orthodoxy" and "cultural modernism," or Republicans and Democrats, or conservatives and liberals. Bringing religion in revealed new dynamics to this story—in particular, a story of religious groups "catching up" to the unaffiliated across generations, at different rates overall, in terms of environmental concern. Again, these manifested themselves as *indirect* (Type 2) religious motives, given the other relationships found in the data. If environmental concern is explained in terms of culture generally, or religion specifically, then visiting differences by gender and social class will more clearly show what types of cultural changes are driving these dynamics within religious groups.

The third reason, which connects to the first and the second, deals specifically with the relationship between race, religion, and politics in the U.S. In particular, Black and white U.S.-Americans differ in numerous ways when it comes to religious belief and practice, as well as tendencies regarding political identity and attitudes. Visiting these at great length would take me too far off course in terms of the focus on the religion–environment connection, but seriously acknowledging these differences means taking race, religious identity, and political party into account at the same time. For example, it is likely that a Black Methodist Democrat is going to be different from a white, religiously unaffiliated Democrat in numerous ways when it comes to cultural issues, and both are likely to be different from a white Methodist who votes Republican. If I am going to seriously disentangle the religion–politics–environment knot, I cannot do so without taking seriously the racial differences, particularly Black–white divides, in the U.S., past and present, in religion, politics, and elsewhere. In the process, I should be able to rule out the possibility that the connection between religion and environmental concern is *really just* (nothing-but?) a connection between politics and environmental concern.

There are three sets of analyses in this chapter. First, I address gender differences in birth cohort dynamics in terms of the religion–environment connection. I do this by dividing the entire data set into women and men (the General Social Survey does not a have a nonbinary gender response option for the years in question, and I am conflating sex and gender here, begging the pardon of fellow gender scholars) to make comparisons. Second, I address differences by social class or social standing. To do this, I divide the entire data set into lower-, middle-, and higher-income groups. This is a simplistic way to divide people up in terms of social class, but because it is a variable I have already used as a *control* in the other models, I can examine more directly how social class shapes the religion–environment connection. The third set of analyses focus on the relationship between race, religion, and political party. The data set is divided into Democrats and Republicans, with the "other party" reference group set aside. I really wanted to focus on the divide between "blue" and "red" here, particularly over the past few decades, for reasons I visit further below. Again, this chapter is a bit more complicated in terms of model-building, but I'll minimize the technical details when I can (for a fuller methodological treatment, see Szrot 2019).

GENDER, RELIGION, AND ENVIRONMENTAL CONCERN

Women tend to be more environmentally concerned than men (McCright and Xiao 2014), but, as figure 5.1 shows, women are also more religious than men. Women and men are very similar in their levels of inspired word Bible belief, but women are notably more likely to be Bible literalists, or persons

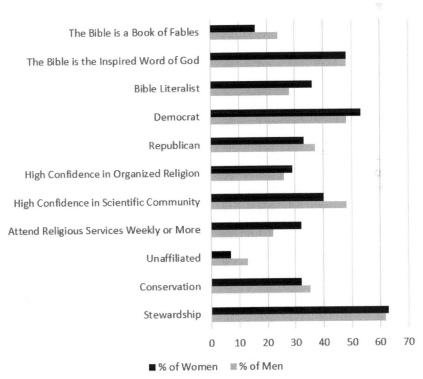

Note: Bible Belief, Conservation only available beginning in 1984, Women N=9,195, Men N=7,492. All other variables 1973-2014, Women N=18,727, Men N=15,539.

Figure 5.1   A Snapshot of Gender Difference.

who believe the Bible is the literal word of God. On the other hand, men are notably more likely than women to believe the Bible is a book of fables. In fact, men are almost twice as likely to identify as unaffiliated, only about two-thirds as likely to report attending religious services weekly or more, have higher confidence in the scientific community, and lower confidence in organized religion. However, women are more likely to identify as Democrats—a party known for tending to be more culturally progressive—and men are more likely to identify as part of the more culturally orthodox and religious Republicans (more on political party differences below). Thus, women are more likely to be more religious than men overall, but are also more closely linked to cultural progressivism, and men are more likely to be secular than women, but are more closely aligned with cultural orthodoxy.

Turning to table 5.1, I have just included the predicted percentages for cohort 0 (the oldest cohort, born before 1905), cohort 4 (the "baby boomers," born between 1950 and 1964), and cohort 6 (the "millennials," born within 1980–1996) to make the table easier to read. As with patterns established in chapter 4, baby boomers differ from millennials far less in environmental concern than from the oldest cohort. Environmental concern increased between the oldest cohort and those born in the mid-twentieth century, into a world in which modern-day "environmentalism" was gaining steam. However, that momentum leveled off somewhat in more recent birth cohorts, once religion is also accounted for.

In terms of stewardship, the overall story is that the "gender gap" in environmental concern has closed over time, with younger women and men being more similar in levels of environmental concern than older cohorts. The exception appears to be Jewish persons, for whom the gender gap remains broad (but Jewish women aren't really different from unaffiliated women in stewardship levels, so I hesitate to make too much of this) and the unaffiliated, among whom the gender gap has actually broadened with younger cohorts. The "gender gap" is narrowest among Catholics, fundamentalist Protestants, and the Nondenominational across all birth cohorts. It has closed quite a bit among Baptists, Methodists, Presbyterians, Lutherans, Episcopalians, moderate and liberal Protestants, and other religious groups.

Conservation tells a somewhat different story, with men being more likely to express a conservation ethic in most groups. The differences between women and men, and relative to the unaffiliated, are not significant in the more theologically liberal groups such as Episcopalians and liberal other Protestants, as well as Jewish persons. The unaffiliated are an exception here, with unaffiliated women expressing more conservation overall than unaffiliated men. Catholic women and men are fairly similar to one another, but differ from the unaffiliated in that Catholic men are more likely than Catholic women to express conservation. Here, the gender gap has not closed among

Table 5.1   Percent Expressing Environmental Concern by Gender, Religion, Cohort

		% Stewardship, Cohort				% Conservation, Cohort			
	%Tot	0	4	6	Sig.	0	4	6	Sig.
Baptist Women	21	21	73	86	***	22	39	40	n/s
Baptist Men	18	34	74	87	*	18	42	47	***
Methodist Women	10	40	76	88	**	17	32	33	***
Methodist Men	9	31	75	89	*	24	41	42	*
Presbyterian Women	4	43	78	89	n/s	22	38	40	n/s
Presbyterian Men	4	36	74	86	n/s	30	34	28	n/s
Lutheran Women	7	37	74	86	***	19	33	35	n/s
Lutheran Men	7	30	73	87	*	25	50	54	*
Episcopalian Women	3	47	81	90	n/s	25	43	44	n/s
Episcopalian Men	2	30	78	91	*	25	46	48	n/s
Nondenom. Women	5	37	74	86	***	21	37	39	n/s
Nondenom. Men	5	34	72	85	n/s	16	42	48	**
Fund. Prot. Women	9	36	73	86	***	19	34	36	**
Fund. Prot. Men	8	35	71	83	n/s	16	41	47	**
Mod. Prot. Women	2	36	73	86	**	18	32	34	n/s
Mod. Prot. Men	2	19	76	92	**	11	37	47	*
Liberal Prot. Women	2	43	78	89	n/s	24	40	42	n/s
Liberal Prot. Men	2	53	81	89	n/s	44	46	38	n/s
Catholic Women	25	39	75	87	***	20	35	37	***
Catholic Men	25	36	74	86	*	22	41	42	**
Jewish Women	2	45	80	90	n/s	18	32	34	*
Jewish Men	2	62	68	70	*	28	38	34	n/s
Other Rel. Women	3	42	78	89	n/s	22	38	40	n/s
Other Rel. Men	4	35	75	88	n/s	37	43	36	n/s
Unaffiliated Women	7	**47**	81	90		**25**	42	44	
Unaffiliated Men	13	**45**	75	85		**39**	45	38	

Note: See Figure 5.1 *Notes* for N Men and Women. Percentages based on 1973–2014 data. Slight variations in 1984–2014 data (see chapter 3 analysis). Cohort 0=before 1905, Cohort 3=1935–1949, Cohort 6=1980–1996. Cohort² main effect (both) and religion*cohort conditional effects (men only) applied to calculate model-predicted percentages. Cohorts 1, 2, 4, and 5 omitted to simplify table.

Controls: Attend Religious Services Weekly or More, High Confidence in Scientific Community, High Confidence in Organized Religion, Education, Race, income, Region, Size of Town/City, Political Party, Feelings about the Bible (Conservation model only).

most groups, and has widened in some. However, some of the most differences appear to be, once again, between unaffiliated women and men, with *higher* conservation levels among unaffiliated women.

Zooming out, bringing religion in complicates the connection between gender and environmental concern. This much is obvious. But why is the gap closing among religious men and women when it comes to stewardship, and not conservation? And why does the gender gap remain relatively wide, or even grow, among the unaffiliated? It would probably help to know that when building the models, in terms of both stewardship and conservation, men were more dynamic overall than women when bringing religion in. That is, even though women are on average more religious than men, men have *changed more* in environmental concern as a function of religion. This means that even though women are more religious, religion is actually *less impor-tant* among women than men when it comes to environmental concern. Other indirect measures like attendance and confidence in organized religion con-firm this pattern—women and men are similar on both measures (see Szrot 2019, 126). But it's the *pattern,* overall, that's interesting, and explaining it means drawing on indirect effects.

Religion, Environment, and Feminism

The "gender divide" fits with the story emerging in the previous chapters: reli-gion has an *indirect* effect on people's environmental attitudes. My argument so far is that religious groups have responded to environmental change. They are both shaped by historical environmental engagement, and have responded to more recent cultural shifts. The mid-twentieth-century U.S. saw the rise of what is referred to as present-day environmentalism, a package of social movements, policies, and concerns that remain influential today. Another cultural shift that took place alongside environmentalism (and incidentally, also has much deeper historical roots dating back to the political enfranchise-ment of women through the abolitionists and suffragists—see Wade and Ferree 2019, 357–70) is the women's movement. Specifically, I argue that a resurgence in demands for the political and economic enfranchisement of women—sometimes called "second-wave feminism"—goes some distance toward explaining the closing of the "gender gap" in environmental concern as a function of religion.

Broadly speaking, as women gained political power and representation within institutions and the broader culture, environmental concern seems to also follow. Overall, women lag far behind men in terms of representation as religious leaders within churches and religious groups, and many of the larg-est religious groups in the U.S. do not currently allow women to be ordained (see Masci 2014). However, it is in the period roughly beginning in the mid-twentieth century that many U.S. religious groups began to ordain women *at all.* These cultural shifts toward empowering women placed pressure on many institutions—including churches and religious organizations—to pro-vide greater opportunities for women. As with environmental concern, these shifts were most dynamic among, and after, the baby boomer generation (born roughly within 1950–1964, cohort 4).

This is only part of the story. The other part involves how the empowerment of women has translated into different policies and perspectives within institutions. Psychologist Steven Pinker (2011) has argued that the *feminization* of political institutions and cultures can lead to greater social stability, as well as lower levels of violence, social dominance, and inequality (684–88). Christina Ergas and Richard York (2012) also found that the status of women is significantly related to carbon dioxide emissions, cross-nationally—feminism is good for the environment. In short, the gender gap has "closed" when it comes to stewardship within many religious groups partly because of the external cultural pressures placed on religious organizations. As women have gained standing outside (and to some extent, within) religious groups, they have indirectly influenced environmental values (such as the levels of environmental concern among men) within those groups. The fact that Catholics and fundamentalist Protestants differ little on environmental issues by gender reinforces this: as groups that have historically been resistant to the cultural shifts associated with second-wave feminism, Catholic and sectarian Protestant men are not "playing catch up" relative to women in terms of environmental issues. Women are more religious than men on average, but religious institutions themselves tend to be dominated by men. Again, religious institutions do not exist in a cultural vacuum. As women gained standing in the broader culture, religious groups responded reflexively to these trends—some by resisting them, and others by embracing them, to varying degrees. Men are more dynamic in their levels of environmental concern as a function of religious group because they are "catching up to" cultural shifts associated with both the empowerment of women and greater environmental concern.

But why are the numbers different on conservation? The "feminization" explanation still holds, to a degree—groups that are more theologically liberal are more likely overall to "lean in to" cultural changes such as those that came with second-wave feminism, and the gender gap tends to be narrower among these groups. But the gap has widened the most among fundamentalist other Protestants, men tend to have higher levels of conservation than women, and a gender gap persists, overall. Surely it cannot just be the cultural pressures associated with the burgeoning women's movement in the case of conservation. I suspect that something deeper in our cultural imagination, connecting "conservation" to "wilderness" and "frontiers," as well as "outdoorsmanship" is complicating the story here. Living in a region in which such outdoor activities are common, and many of them take place against a background of national parks and outdoor recreation, that many of these activities most associated with wilderness tend to be dominated by men is readily apparent. Conservation as measured here is a place where those who hunt and fish might find common ground with bird-watchers, hikers, and urban environmentalists, potentially tilting the gender dynamic. Stewardship, as measured here, less so. However, future trends toward the enfranchisement of women may lead to differing dynamics in this regard as well, with women becoming increasingly likely to participate in the cultural activities associated with conservation.

Such trends may already be apparent among the unaffiliated, where women notably outpace men in conservation in more recent cohorts. The gender gap has widened a bit among unaffiliated women and men in terms of steward-ship, but narrowed and then widened in terms of conservation. In both cases, women outpaced men in environmental concern. The simplest explanation for this (and the simplest explanation is to be favored, of course, barring good reasons to think it is seriously incomplete) is that the changes in religious institutions as reflexive responses to empowerment of women in the broader culture simply are not happening among the unaffiliated. The reason for the gender gap in the unaffiliated can likely be explained in terms of political views and other secular factors. For example, figure 5.1 shows that men are more likely to vote Republican than women, on average, and this is a con-sistent negative predictor of environmental concern. It remains possible that the reasons why women and men disaffiliate, or identify as unaffiliated, are different, potentially driving this as well as other gender gaps.

To sum up, I argue that both the women's movement and long-standing environmental imaginations have collaborated to produce these dynamics within religious groups. Bringing religion into the gender–environment conversations shows how religious organizations can, and do, reflexively respond to cultural as well as environmental changes—by embracing, or resisting, them, to varying degrees. When it comes to stewardship, the gender gap closes when bringing religion in—men tend to catch up to women in the younger cohorts. Regarding conservation, men tend to out-pace women, with some noteworthy exceptions (such as the unaffiliated). Centering the role of gender in religion–environment conversations adds more depth and nuance to how environmental imaginations may themselves be gendered, as well as how a cultural connection between the enfranchise-ment of women and cultivation of greater environmental concern occurs intergenerationally. Religious groups are surely gendered institutions, being a potent source of rules and norms in terms of what women, men, and those of all genders are expected to do (and not do). But they are also reflexive, and changes in gender rules and norms may, to varying degrees, permeate religious organizations. In this broader cultural context of changing gender expectations, people also "do" gender reflexively, considering what rules to follow, bend—or break. The dance of ideas, from persons and interactions to institutions to broader historical and cultural currents, recurs and begins anew.

INCOME, RELIGION, AND
ENVIRONMENTAL CONCERN

I do not think it would be an exaggeration to argue that the ongoing enfranchisement of women since the mid-twentieth century has changed the world in
countless ways, and continues to do so. In the previous section, I showed how
and why that matters in terms of the religion–environment connection. However,
the enfranchisement of women did not take place in a vacuum, either, both stir-
ring and being stirred by another set of changes that took place outside religious
organizations in the U.S. and elsewhere. Some scholars have referred to this as
a transition to *post-industrial society*—a society which is increasingly shaped
by interactions between people and services rather than nature and industry (see
Bell 1996, 147–55). Others have argued that this transition is better understood
as a doubling down or speeding up of industrial capitalism (see Harvey 1990;
Jameson 1984). Still others have pointed to this change as one characterized by
risks both created and detected by human activity, and reflexive responses to it
(see Beck 1992; Giddens 1990, 2000). All have some purchase on understanding
the period in which these changes have unfolded, though I tend toward the risk
and reflexivity conceptualization for most of the themes in this work.

What each of these has in common is an implicit, or explicit, affirmation of the
secularization axiom—that religion is "going away" or has "gone away already,"
that it has lost or is losing practical importance or moral authority. There has been
erosion of religious belief and practice in some parts of the world, some much
more so than others. Given this section's focus on political and economic themes,
it is worth briefly considering *why* that might be taking place. Here, political
scientists Pippa Norris and Ronald Inglehart (2011) argue, using data and models
that account for change over time, that there is a meaningful relationship between
the *existential security* of a society and how religious it is. That is, societies that
are healthier, wealthier, safer, and more educated on average also tend to become
less religious over time. The U.S. is more religious than other wealthy countries,
according to this perspective, because it has higher levels of social inequality than
other wealthy countries, and prioritizes the relative precarity of individual initia-
tive and entrepreneurship over the relative security of state-funded social welfare
and safety nets (Norris and Inglehart 2011, 83–110).

This raises a common point of confusion in public conversation, particularly among critics of religion. Societies that are more religious also tend to
be poorer, sicker, more dangerous, and less educated, but this isn't *because*
religion makes them this way. Instead, people are more likely to turn to,
and hang onto, religious ways of understanding the world when they come
of age in an *existentially insecure* setting—when they feel more vulnerable
to things that seem beyond their control, and feel the future is uncertain or
largely beyond their grasp. The explanation was meant to capture differences

between countries, but it's possible that this explains why persons within a society who are more existentially vulnerable (such as lower-income U.S.-Americans, persons of color, and older persons) may also tend to be more religious. It's also possible that this is why women in the U.S. are more religious than men on many measures in this study: the oldest cohorts of women in this study were born before women had the right to vote (1920, a century ago, women were granted the right to vote nationwide), and grew up in an America where the economic, social, cultural, and other liberties of women were formally or informally restricted.

Another facet of vulnerability has to do with environmental conditions, or hazards. *Environmental justice* scholars and advocates argue that environmental hazards tend to be felt most strongly by those in a society with the least political and economic power, such as women, racial/ethnic minorities, and low-income persons (see Harlan et al. 2015). Connecting the dots, those who are more likely to be affected by environmental problems are also those who are more likely to be religious. It remains to be seen, however, whether or not this translates into higher, or lower, levels of environmental concern as a function of both income and religious group.

Based on figure 5.2, results are more mixed than existential security theory would suggest. Bible belief indicates that high-income persons are more likely than others to view the Bible as a book of fables written by men, or as the inspired word of God, but are notably less likely to identify as Bible literalists. Bible literalists are more likely to be low-income people, but overall, middle-income people are least likely to view the Bible as a book of fables. In terms of Bible belief, high-income people are the least religious, and middle-income people are the most religious. Confidence in organized religion is also slightly higher among middle-income persons, as is the percentage of people who attend religious services weekly or more. High-income persons are more likely to be Republican, and to have high confidence in the scientific community, whereas low-income persons are more likely to be Democrats. Slightly higher levels of both conservation and stewardship are found among low-income persons. Overall, middle-income persons are more religious. This snapshot of the groups is also a bit more nuanced in practice when it comes to both stewardship and conservation, as noted in table 5.2.

There are more significant differences by religious group among high-income people. However, where there are significant differences, they are negative. That is, high-income religious people tend to be less environmentally concerned in terms of stewardship than high-income unaffiliated persons. Overall, however, middle-income persons are more dynamic. Middle-income persons in the youngest cohort tend to be more likely to express stewardship than low- or high-income persons of the same religious group, but this effect is only found among Protestants—*all Protestant groups* except fundamentalist

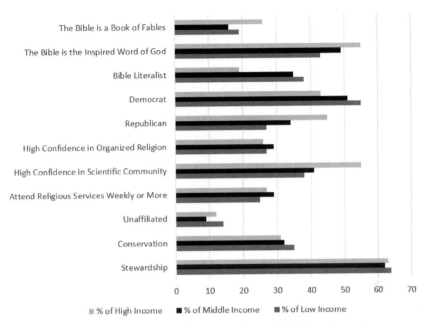

The Bible is a Book of Fables
The Bible is the Inspired Word of God
Bible Literalist
Democrat
Republican
High Confidence in Organized Religion
High Confidence in Scientific Community
Attend Religious Services Weekly or More
Unaffiliated
Conservation
Stewardship

0   10   20   30   40   50   60   70

▨ % of High Income   ■ % of Middle Income   ■ % of Low Income

Note: Bible Belief, Conservation only available beginning in 1984, Below Average Income N=5,143, Average Income N=7,762, Above Average Income N=3,782. All other variables 1973-2014, Below Average Income N=9,916, Average Income N=16,873, Above Average Income N=7,477

Figure 5.2   A Snapshot of Differences by Income.

other Protestants, for whom low- and middle-income persons don't differ. Catholics show no difference by income group in the youngest cohort, the unaffiliated differ by only two points (with lowest levels among middle-income unaffiliated persons), and among both Jewish persons and other religious groups, middle-income persons have the lowest levels of stewardship. To summarize, there is something of a "coming apart" effect happening by income levels among Protestants in particular, with lowest levels of stewardship tending to be found among high-income persons, and highest levels of stewardship to be found among middle-income persons. Low-income persons tend to have middling levels of stewardship, and don't differ that much from one another in terms of stewardship in the same religious group. This means three things: first, low-income people are more similar to one another overall in terms of stewardship regardless of religious group. Second, high-income *Protestants* tend to be more similar overall in having *lower* levels of stewardship than the unaffiliated and other religious groups. Third, changes in stewardship across cohorts have been most dynamic among middle-income Protestants, so that consistently higher levels of stewardship are tend to be found among middle-income Protestants in the youngest cohort.

Table 5.2   Percent Expressing Environmental Concern by Income, Religion, Cohort

	%Tot	% Stewardship, Cohort				% Conservation, Cohort			
		0	4	6	Sig.	0	4	6	Sig.
Baptist Low Inc	23	36	66	71	*	19	47	45	n/s
Baptist Mid Inc	21	33	69	75	**	26	40	43	n/s
Baptist High Inc	12	33	62	67	***	28	40	42	n/s
Methodist Low Inc	8	37	67	72	n/s	15	41	39	n/s
Methodist Mid Inc	10	37	72	76	n/s	23	36	38	*
Methodist High Inc	10	36	65	71	**	28	39	41	n/s
Presbyterian Low Inc	3	40	70	74	n/s	18	45	43	n/s
Presbyterian Mid Inc	4	40	73	77	n/s	27	41	44	n/s
Presbyterian High Inc	6	37	65	71	*	38	51	54	n/s
Lutheran Low Inc	5	33	63	68	**	14	37	36	*
Lutheran Mid Inc	7	31	70	77	**	25	38	41	n/s
Lutheran High Inc	7	36	64	70	**	35	48	50	n/s
Episcopalian Low Inc	2	40	70	74	n/s	23	53	51	n/s
Episcopalian Mid Inc	2	48	78	82	n/s	27	41	44	n/s
Episcopalian High Inc	4	38	66	72	n/s	32	44	47	n/s
Nondenom. Low Inc	5	34	64	69	*	18	46	44	n/s
Nondenom. Mid Inc	5	35	69	74	n/s	28	41	44	n/s
Nondenom High Inc	5	32	60	66	***	24	35	37	**
Fund. Prot. Low Inc	10	36	66	71	*	15	40	38	*
Fund. Prot. Mid Inc	10	34	67	71	*	25	39	41	n/s
Fund. Prot. High Inc	7	30	58	64	***	28	40	42	n/s
Mod. Prot. Low Inc	1	36	66	71	n/s	10	28	27	*
Mod. Prot. Mid Inc	1	26	72	82	**	24	37	39	n/s
Mod. Prot. High Inc	1	27	54	60	***	32	44	47	n/s
Liberal Prot. Low Inc	1	43	72	76	n/s	19	47	45	n/s
Liberal Prot. Mid Inc	2	38	76	82	n/s	29	43	46	n/s
Liberal Prot. High Inc	3	49	75	80	n/s	37	49	52	n/s
Catholic Low Inc	23	37	66	71	*	16	42	41	*
Catholic Mid Inc	26	40	68	71	n/s	25	38	41	n/s
Catholic High Inc	25	37	66	71	**	29	41	43	n/s
Jewish Low Inc	1	31	60	66	n/s	16	42	41	n/s
Jewish Mid Inc	1	60	65	57	*	25	38	41	*
Jewish High Inc	5	42	70	75	n/s	29	41	43	n/s
Other Rel. Low Inc	4	40	70	74	n/s	18	46	44	n/s
Other Rel. Mid Inc	3	45	70	71	n/s	25	38	41	n/s
Other Rel. High Inc	4	42	70	75	n/s	31	43	45	n/s
Unaffiliated Low Inc	14	**41**	70	75		20	48	46	
Unaffiliated Mid Inc	9	**47**	72	73		28	41	44	
Unaffiliated High Inc	12	**44**	72	77		34	47	49	

Turning to conservation levels, the pattern is a bit different. In this case, high-income people tend to have higher levels of conservation than middle- or lower-income people in the same religious group. This effect is, once again, among Protestants more so than other groups. However, when comparing the oldest cohort to younger cohorts, it is middle-income people overall who have been the most dynamic, slowly "catching up" to higher income people of the same religious group. Most of these effects are not significant, suggesting that a large part of the differences in conservation can be explained in terms of income differences instead of religious differences. In other words, income exerts some meaningful effects on the religion–environment connection in both cases, but plays a stronger and more consistent role overall in conservation.

Religion and Environment: Who Must, Who Can, and Who Wants To

Fitting this information into the bigger picture, institutionalized reflexivity has taken place most clearly and consistently among middle-income people. Environmental concern, as measured here, and as cultivated over time in religious groups, is being cultivated most consistently among the middle classes. Even though it is high-income Protestants that, in the youngest cohort, actually end up with higher levels of conservation levels on average, middle-income Protestants have changed the most from the oldest to the youngest cohort. This complicates a picture of *existential security* in the case of religion—whereby religion is lower on average among people with higher incomes—and *environmental injustice* in the case of environmental concern, whereby those who are low-income would be more expected to be more concerned about environmental changes/impacts they are more likely to personally experience.

The simplest explanation I can offer is that low-income people become environmentally concerned because they *have to,* middle-income people, because they *can,* and high-income people, because they (don't) *want to.* Low-income people, and especially low-income persons of color (more below), are more vulnerable to environmental hazards (Harlan et al. 2015). They are more likely to live in areas where severe weather events are going to have greater impacts (Chakraborty et al. 2019), more likely to live in or near areas that lack consistent access to clean water (McDonald and Jones 2018), and are more threatened by industrial waste (Mohai et al. 2009). This accounts for why low-income people have slightly higher environmental concern overall, and also why religion doesn't matter that much *among* low-income people. Factors other than religion are at work in fostering environmental concern.

For middle-income people, having more economic resources to draw from allows people to participate in more voluntary organizations and groups, and to raise children in environments that provide more access to social networks where a pro-environmental *habitus* is more likely to grow. Religious institutions may have more resources to place emphasis on environmental issues when they are attended (and funded) by people with more income to spare. This fits with some of the earliest research on the religion–environment connection: Yaple (1982) found that a lot of religious leaders wanted to do more to be "green," but had to balance such concerns behind other priorities such as ministry and charitable outreach. Additionally, people who commit themselves to being more active in cultivating faith-based environmental concern may find themselves fighting uphill battles amid shifting cultural and economic priorities in religious organizations (see Baugh 2017; Ellingson 2016). This also fits with the interplay of *habitus, reflexivity,* and environmental change that I have offered throughout this work, and gives further reasons why people (particularly the middle classes) hold higher levels of environmental concern that are *indirectly* related to religious identity and upbringing.

High-income people simply have different priorities on average when it comes to both religion and the environment. Note that high-income people overall have lower levels of conservation, but that high-income *Protestants* are more likely to express conservation. At the same time, stewardship tends to be lower among high-income Protestants than middle-income persons of the same religious group. High-income people, particularly high-income Protestants, hold a range of different cultural and economic priorities on average. Conservation may have a greater significance for high-income people because it is tied to symbols of cultural and national identity such as national parks, and also serves as a space for recreation among upper-middle-class urban and suburban dwellers. Both factors are also consistent with earlier findings showing that more strictly religious people in some cases tended to hold higher levels of conservation, but this does not explain why Republicans score consistently lower on conservation than Independents or Democrats. Stewardship is more closely tied to *environmentalism* which may "turn off" a group of people that are more likely to self-identify as Republicans. In this regard, there is something of the "culture war" effect here, such that high-income people's cultural and economic priorities may be at odds with what they take *stewardship* to mean. *Environmentalism* is associated with culturally progressive ideas, and calls to "improve and protect the environment" may also involve more progressive taxation and regulation requiring increased economic sacrifices by high-income persons. Of course, I can test these explanations more directly by looking at politics, which is where I'm headed next.

POLITICS, RACE, RELIGION, AND
ENVIRONMENTAL CONCERN

As I mentioned above, it would be difficult to talk about religion and politics without also talking about race. Put simply, there are some major cultural and historical differences that cut across both politics and religion in the U.S., particularly the divide between Black and white U.S.-Americans on both fronts.

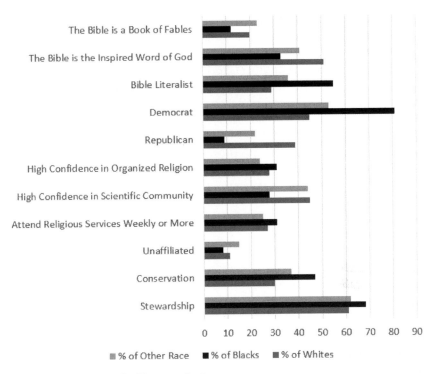

Figure 5.3 Snapshot of Differences by Race.

This is easier to see by looking at race rather than politics first, which is what I have done in figure 5.3. The data only accounted for three possibilities in terms of race: Black, white, and other. This is useful for making some big comparisons, particularly between Blacks and whites, but is too simplistic to say much about the full racial diversity of the U.S., past and present. First, over half of Blacks are Bible literalists, compared to less than 30 percent of whites. Second, over 80 percent of Blacks identify as, or lean, Democrat, and less than 10 percent identify as, or lean, Republican. Blacks are more likely on average to be more confident in organized religion, less confident in science, more likely to attend religious services weekly or more, less likely to be unaffiliated, and much more likely to express both conservation and stewardship. This religious, cultural, political, and environmental distinctiveness makes for an interesting set of comparisons.

Model-Building in Red and Blue

Before diving into the comparisons, I should make another note about the process of model-building. Again, the model-building process involves a dialogue, asking a series of questions to figure out what factors fit better, or what factors can be taken out without making the model any "less bad" at predicting the outcome (in this case, environmental concern). So, if I'm going to look at both race and politics at the same time, I'm going to end up with some more complicated models than I had in the previous chapters, in terms of the number of things that can be happening. First, I divided the data into Democrats and Republicans and then set aside the rest. Other political party, the reference group for a lot of the other work I've done so far, isn't a good group for *within-group* comparisons because there are simply too many reasons a person might not identify as a Republican or a Democrat. People who are *other* might be centrists who are willing to vote for Democrats sometimes and Republicans other times. They might also be members of the Green party, libertarians, socialists, and so on. These differences are, well, *too different* to accurately examine on their own without more information, and most of these ideologically diverse groups are too small to gather a lot of data on with "big-picture" statistics (see the discussion in chapter 4 on the limitations of big pictures). On the other hand, comparing the Blue Team and the Red Team, the Democrats and the Republicans, established, mainstream political parties that have fairly clear platforms and priorities, should yield interesting results.

Within the Blue and Red Teams, I still have race, religion, and birth cohort all potentially playing a role. This means that there can be differences by race, by religion, and by birth cohort. In chapter 4, I was operating under the assumption (confirmed by the models) that different religious groups changed differently across birth cohorts in terms of stewardship and conservation. That is, looking at religion-by-cohort was better at predicting environmental concern on both measures than just looking at religion and at cohort separately. In this chapter, when I looked at gender, it turned out that this assumption held for men but not for women. For men, the religion-by-cohort effect made the model better. For women, it didn't, and so I just looked at religion and cohort separately for women. In the income model, the religion-by-cohort effect only made the model better for middle-income people. For low-income and high-income people, it didn't, so I just looked at religion and cohort separately for these groups.

For these models, I had to test a lot more things. I not only tested whether different religious groups overall might change differently by birth cohort (religion-by-cohort—they did). I also had to test whether different races within the same religion might be different from one another (race-by-religion), whether different races overall might change differently by birth cohort (race-by-cohort), and finally, whether different races within the same religion might change differently by birth cohort (race-by-religion-by-cohort). If you're a model-builder, this might sound like a fun challenge. If you're not, this might already be giving you a headache. To sum up, there are a lot of different ways that race, religion, and birth cohort can interact with one another within a political party in relation to both stewardship and conservation. The charts I've presented below are the outcome of testing many different terms and effects, and omitting the ones that didn't help the models fit better. For more details on this, see Szrot (2019, 164–97).

Race, Religion, and Environmental Injustice in the U.S.

In the U.S., the racial divides between whites on one hand, and Blacks, Indigenous peoples, and other persons of color on the other, are evident. These divides extend to both religion and the environment. Regarding religion, an enduring divide which both shapes and is shaped by culturally and historically distinctive experiences of whites and Blacks in the U.S. cuts across the lines of religious groups which have been examined in this work, particularly regarding Protestantism. When deciding how to look more closely at race and politics in terms of the religion–environment connection, I almost immediately discovered that many of the historical religious groups in this study, such as Lutherans, Presbyterians, and Episcopalians, included very few Blacks or people of color. Other groups, such as Baptists, Methodists, and the Nondenominational were much more racially heterogeneous. This is not my first foray into the study of religion, in which I have confronted the enduring racial divide in terms of U.S.-American religion. I have read the scathing 1963 declaration of Martin Luther King, Jr.: "We must face the fact that in America, the church is still the most segregated institution in America. At 11:00 on Sunday morning when we stand and sing, and 'Christ has no East or West,' we stand at the most segregated hour in this nation" (quoted in Jones 2016, 164).

Scholars in the sociology of religion have detailed this "religious divide" in many ways. Those who have tried to study multiracial religious congregations in the U.S. have found that such congregations remain rare in the twenty-first century (Emerson and Woo 2006). Others have encountered resistance from religious leaders in studying race relations among Christians (Shelton and Emerson 2012, 17–8). Still others have shown how racial divisions in Christianity predate the Civil War, resulting in rich—and distinctive—religious beliefs, practices, politics, and worldviews (see Emerson and Smith 2000; Shelton and Emerson 2012). *To what extent do these cultural and religious distinctions translate into different responses to environmental change?*

To ask this question is to invite another: *how does race factor into experiences of environmental change, and the hazards that come with it?* In one case study after another, Robert Bullard's *Unequal Protection* (1994) showed how African Americans, Indigenous peoples, and persons of color in the U.S.

have faced multiple and enduring *environmental injustices.* Environmental hazards such as landfills and toxic industrial sites tend to be located in areas that are more heavily populated with people of color, as well as low-income/ working-class people. The reasons for this are complex, but undoubtedly are related to a legacy of decades of racial segregation, enforced both officially and unofficially in U.S. cities (Mohai et al. 2009; Rothstein 2017). Somewhat ironically, these trends may have been accelerated by the rise of mainstream environmentalism in the U.S. after the 1960s. Relatively affluent, white communities have leveraged social, economic, and political power to more successfully keep hazardous waste sites out of their neighborhoods—at the expense of neighborhoods populated by working-class people and persons of color (Mohai and Saha 2006, 2007; Saha and Mohai 2005). As environmental justice scholar-activists Robert Bullard and Beverly Hendrix Wright (1987) argued, "not in my backyard" (NIMBY) gave way to "place in Blacks' back-yards" (PIBBY).

Interestingly, one of the earliest, and most groundbreaking, works on environmental justice was commissioned by the United Church of Christ Commission for Racial Justice: *Toxic Wastes and Race in the United States,* which concluded that race was the strongest predictor of where toxic waste sites were located in the U.S. (Chavis and Lee 1987). A common theme among faith-based environmental groups and organizations has also been addressing the human dimensions of environmental change, with a focus on recruiting persons of color, rural, and low-income populations—those whose voices have more often been muted by a predominantly white, suburban, politically progressive, middle-class environmentalism (see Baugh 2017; Ellingson 2016). In other words, an analysis such as this would be incomplete without delving into the themes of race, particularly the Black–white divide, at the religion–environment intersection.

RELIGION AND ENVIRONMENTAL CONCERN: BLACK AND WHITE, RED AND BLUE

Table 5.3 sums up the results of this model-building process. There are several things to note before I start really analyzing the information in table 5.3. First, the percentage of the total, or %Tot, column reports the market share of the religious group *among Democrats* in total, rather than breaking down the percentages by race. This is to keep the focus on religious groups, and also because breaking down the data further would have resulted in many percentages of the total that were below 1 percent. Second, Presbyterians, Lutherans, Episcopalians, liberal and moderate other Protestants, Jewish persons, and other religious groups were not subdivided by race. This was an analytical

Table 5.3 **Percent Expressing Environmental Concern by Race, Politics, Religion, Cohort**

	%Tot	% Stewardship, Cohort				% Conservation, Cohort			
		0	4	6	Sig.	0	4	6	Sig.
Black Baptist Dem.	22	34	69	76	***	12	38	43	***
White Baptist Dem		49	69	70	**	37	52	46	**
Other Baptist Dem		26	60	68	*	17	32	42	*
Baptist Republican	17	29	59	66	n/s	29	48	59	*
Black Methodist Dem	9	36	68	74	**	12	36	40	**
White Methodist Dem		42	73	78	**	39	41	30	*
Other Methodist Dem		49	78	83	*	20	20	21	*
Methodist Republican	12	34	65	71	*	33	34	34	n/s
Presbyterian Dem	3	35	73	81	**	28	43	38	n/s
Presbyterian Repub.	6	33	64	70	n/s	45	27	19	n/s
Lutheran Democrat	5	33	72	80	***	13	42	48	*
Lutheran Repub.	9	28	58	65	n/s	29	54	66	*
Episcopalian Dem	2	50	78	83	n/s	28	43	38	n/s
Episcopalian Rep	3	32	63	69	n/s	29	30	30	n/s
Black Nonden. Dem	4	46	85	91	*	40	65	64	**
White Nonden. Dem		39	81	89	*	6	60	81	n/s
Other Nonden. Dem		13	51	65	**	21	27	31	n/s
Nonden. Republican	6	25	54	61	n/s	35	43	47	n/s
Black Fund. Prot Dem	8	32	68	76	**	5	34	49	***
White Fund. Prot Dem		57	71	69	**	34	46	39	***
Other Fund. Prot Dem		28	64	72	*	23	29	33	**
Fund. Prot Republican	10	27	56	63	*	37	45	49	n/s
Other Prot Democrat	1	31	76	86	**	17	29	25	*
Other Prot Repub.	2	26	56	62	n/s	29	30	30	n/s
Liberal Prot Democrat	1	31	64	71	*	30	45	40	n/s
Liberal Prot Rep	2	36	67	73	*	29	30	30	n/s
Catholic Democrat	27	40	69	73	**	23	36	31	***
Catholic Republican	22	32	63	69	n/s	17	18	18	*
Jewish Democrat	3	58	67	63	n/s	20	32	28	**
Jewish Republican	1	30	60	66	n/s	29	30	30	n/s
Other Religion Dem	4	51	72	73	n/s	24	38	33	*
Other Religion Rep	3	33	64	70	n/s	29	30	30	n/s
Black Unaffil. Dem	11	**58**	77	77	n/s	30	45	39	***
White Unaffil. Dem		**56**	75	76		39	55	50	
Other Unaffil Dem		**52**	72	73		29	30	30	
Unaffil Republican	7	**30**	60	67		48	46	46	

decision based on the lack of racial diversity within groups. The Protestant groups I mentioned simply had too few Blacks or persons of color to say much about them—again, birth cohort numbers at or near zero would damage the integrity of the analysis. Also, Judaism is, like other world religions, an ethnicity as well as a religion, so it doesn't make sense to divide Jewish persons into U.S.-specific racial categories like *Black, white,* and *other*. I could say something similar about the *other religion* group—because the meanings of, and distinctions between, race, ethnicity, and religion vary by world religion, mapping U.S.-specific divisions onto this diverse group would produce some artificial and potentially meaningless results. Of course, being a Black Muslim, rather than a Muslim immigrant from the Middle East, may mean differences that would be fascinating and illuminating to disentangle in terms of environmental concern, but I do not have a large enough sample of either group to do this here.

Furthermore, Republicans are not further subdivided by race. Figure 5.3 shows that a relatively small minority of Blacks (less than 10 percent) and other racial groups (about 22 percent) identify as or lean Republican. However, race was ultimately omitted from the Republican models because the models "told" me during their construction that the conditional effects of race (race-by-religion, race-by-religion-by-cohort) didn't make the model any better at predicting either stewardship or conservation among Republicans. In other words, the models for predicting stewardship and conservation among Republicans are simpler than the models for predicting stewardship and conservation among Democrats. In fact, a great deal of the complexity at the intersection of race, religion, and birth cohort is limited to Democrats and those who lean Democrat. Republicans are more similar to one another in terms of environmental concern, even as a function of religious group and race.

Religious Republicans, overall, don't differ that much from unaffiliated Republicans, and several of the effects are not statistically significant for either stewardship or conservation. This does not mean that the religion–environment connection is *nothing but* political party. For one thing, there are similar upward trends by birth cohort among both Republicans and Democrats overall. This means, contrary to the debates about culture wars and polarization, Republicans as a function of religion and birth cohort are in many ways catching up to Democrats, at least among the more racially diverse religious groups. The resistance to environmental issues, where and when it exists, is more likely to be found among older Republicans and older cohorts; there is a negative relationship between age and environmental concern, as well as the positive relationship between voting Republican and being older. It is also noteworthy that both parties have changed directions in terms of their overall party platforms, respectively. According to Jones (2016), this transformation took place beginning in the 1960s, when disaffected white Democrat voters, especially from the South, shifted into the Republican party in response to growing acceptance of Civil Rights among Democrats (88). However, identity in terms of political party is more likely to manifest itself as a *year effect* rather than a *cohort effect*. People are not born Republicans or Democrats in the same ways as they are born into religious groups, and existing research on change over time shows that political and economic views are less durable than moral or cultural dimensions (see Vaisey and Lizardo 2016). In other words, political party affiliation does not explain away religious effects across birth cohort—nor should it be expected to, because political and religious dimensions of life arise at different times in the life course (though they can be, and are, of course related in other ways).

There is another trend among Republicans that is present in stewardship models, if less so in conservation models. That is, among the historically white religious groups (those that are not subdivided by race), Democrats and Republicans have both increased in stewardship across the cohort, but are moving apart relative to one another. In these groups, younger Republicans are not catching up to younger Democrats; they are falling behind them. This, coupled with the relationship between age, religion, and political party, suggests the following: *it is among historically white Protestant religious groups, specifically, that Republicans most depart from Democrats in terms of stewardship.* The youngest cohort Catholic, Jewish, and other religion groups differ little in stewardship levels. Conservation is a little more complicated. Baptist Republicans in the youngest cohort actually have higher levels of conservation than any of the Democrat groups, and Republicans also outpace Democrats among Lutherans. Catholics, on the other hand, show a great deal of distance between Democrats and Republicans at the most recent cohort. In most other cases, the religious groups do not differ significantly from the unaffiliated. Among Democrats in racially diverse religious groups, the trend seems to be toward catching up, with the youngest cohorts being fairly similar by race when it comes to conservation. Again, making political party a central part of this analysis affects the results, but does not negate them.

Black Protestant groups differ from their white counterparts in that they are more both intergenerationally dynamic overall and express higher levels of environmental concern in younger cohorts. Blacks are more dynamic in stewardship as well as conservation (with the exception to the dynamics of the Nondenominational and conservation), and (with the exception of Methodists in stewardship, and Baptists in conservation) outpace their white counterparts in environmental concern among cohort 6. Though there are some trends toward lower levels of environmental concern among whites in more sectarian or theologically fundamentalist groups, such trends are absent among blacks. Maybe, to some degree, environmental concern has been a "casualty of the culture wars," given consistent partisan divides, and some theological tendencies, but this story is inconsistent. It does not hold up very well across generations, and where it does hold true, it is only among white Protestants in historically white Protestant religious groups. Blacks, as well as whites in more diverse religious groups, regardless of overall theological tendencies, are *more* environmentally engaged overall. This is especially true of whites who vote, or lean, Democrat, but the ideological gaps are narrower in these groups than in the historically white Protestant groups.

Other race results are rather inconsistent overall. In some groups, such as the Methodists, other racial groups have outpaced both Blacks and whites in stewardship. In other groups, such as fundamentalist Protestants and the Nondenominational, other racial groups have fallen far behind both blacks and whites in conservation. I stress here that this is a limitation of "big pictures." The group *other race* includes persons of Asian and Latin American descent, as well as persons from the Middle East, and Indigenous persons—all racial and ethnic groups that identify as neither Black nor white. Understanding the diverse results for this group would mean zooming in with interviews or field work at the level of neighborhoods or congregations rather than broad religious groups. However, the diversity of results here shows clearly that a story about religion, or politics, is incomplete insofar as it does not take race into account.

One final comparison involves the unaffiliated. Again, confirming some earlier findings, race doesn't matter as much in terms of stewardship—the unaffiliated are separated by only a few percentage points. Even though unaffiliated Republicans express lower levels of stewardship, they are only six percentage points from other race unaffiliated Democrats. Given that the unaffiliated are much more likely be white, and to vote/lean Democrat, race and party overall appear to be less important than being religiously unaffiliated overall. Note, however, that the unaffiliated have only middling levels of stewardship compared to many religious groups—especially those religious groups that are racially diverse. Black fundamentalist Protestants who vote/lean Democrat in cohort 6, for example, have similar levels of stewardship to white unaffiliated Democrats. In terms of conservation, the story differs quite a bit, with unaffiliated Blacks and other racial groups who vote/lean Democrat being far less likely than their white counterparts, as well as Republicans, to express conservation.

Divided on Religion and Environmental Concern: Where, When, and Why

What does this mean more broadly, however? There are a lot of numbers to sift through, but there are some key takeaways here. The first is that Republicans aren't that different from one another overall, in terms of environmental concern (with a few exceptions), but across birth cohorts, Republicans have increased in environmental concern in general. The second is that the groups that are moving apart along party lines tend to be historically white Protestant groups as opposed to racially diverse religious groups.

Connecting these ideas together, bringing religion into the race–politics–environment connection provides a lot more data, but also tends to simplify the picture in important ways. Younger cohorts with few exceptions are more environmentally concerned than older cohorts; millennials are less different from baby boomers than baby boomers are from the oldest cohorts. Religious groups with histories of environmental concern have tended to "catch up to" the unaffiliated with younger cohorts.

There is a real divide between Republicans and Democrats on environmental issues, and I don't intend to deny that here. That divide is growing. However, when bringing religion in, it becomes clearer that the divide is only indirectly due to the culture wars. Environmental concern is a casualty of broader cultural alignments, and only inconsistently so. The divide is not a divide between Blue and Red, nor between the pious and the unbelieving. It is not a divide between Black and white, either. It is a divide that takes place primarily *within* historically white Protestant churches, and between younger and older Republican cohorts.

These trends are connected to one another, and fit into the bigger story, as well. Divides within historically white Protestant churches, such that younger Republicans and younger Democrats have moved apart, should be placed alongside the fact that many of the denominations within these religious groups are both *aging* and *shrinking* (see, for example, Jones 2016). That is, they have tended to lose membership over the last 50 years, and those who remain committed to these religious groups tend to be older than the average age of the population. This means young people who remain committed to these religious groups as adults—who have not disaffiliated or switched—worship alongside older populations. They are therefore more likely to be "plugged into" a social network that is older, overall, and if they also already lean or identify as Republican, they are sure to find sympathetic fellows.

On the other hand, because these are typically religious groups that have both incorporated environmental concern into their fold through historical doctrine and engagement, and also groups that contain theologically moderate and liberal elements, it is also possible for younger members of these churches to find and reinforce social networks with others who worship alongside them, tilt Blue politically, and therefore are more likely to have access to the social resources to foster and strengthen environmental concern. This is another example of how religious groups may *indirectly* work to foster environmental attitudes through social networks and opportunities for interpersonal engagement. Social networks play an important role in fostering and strengthening beliefs over time, and in the U.S., churches have historically played an important role in fostering social ties. This likely also explains in part why there are racial differences in environmental concern by religious group—the distinctiveness of churches in the U.S. has been shaped by historical racial tensions, particularly between Black and white U.S.-Americans, such that the experiences within Black Protestant churches differ in myriad ways from white churches, as well as by the environmental injustices that have disproportionately fallen upon persons of color in the U.S.

CHAPTER SUMMARY: PLOT TWISTS AND RESOLUTION

Even a story built around numbers and logic needs some plot twists. In this chapter, I wanted to see if the story that unfolded in chapters 3 and 4 could withstand some real challenges, and even grow in the process. Bringing in some of the most significant lines of research from my home discipline, sociology—race, class, and gender—and also a factor that seemed likely to mess with my conclusions—political party differences—added new dimensions. Overall, the story has changed in a few ways, but I'll start with the "big-picture" ways in which it hasn't. With very few exceptions, younger cohorts are more environmentally concerned than older cohorts, but that tends to level off with cohort 4, which I have sometimes referred to simply as the baby boomers (1950–1964), and grows at a somewhat slower pace after that. This is largely true regardless of what other variables are thrown into the mix. More, and more dynamic, environmental concern is still found in the groups that have a history of engaging with environmental issues, such as Baptists, Methodists, Presbyterians, Lutherans, Episcopalians, and Catholics. Lower numbers tend to be found among sectarian Protestants (fundamentalist other Protestants) but this isn't consistent, and bringing in gender, social class, race, and politics shows that it isn't *because* of theological fundamentalism. Baptists are largely theologically fundamentalist, as well, and they are among the more dynamic groups in terms of environmental concern, with Black Baptists being even more so.

  Gender, income, and racial differences do have some complicating effects, though. Turns out men have been more dynamic than women when bringing religion in. I have argued that this is typically because men are "catching up to" women in levels of stewardship within the same religious group due to broader cultural shifts (the political and economic empowerment of women via second-wave feminism alongside the burgeoning environmentalism movement). This timetable coincides with the earlier timetables. If environmentalism could be said to be a product of the 1960s, the same could be said for a resurgence of the women's movement. Betty Friedan's (1963) keystone work *The Feminine Mystique* was published a year after Rachel Carson's (2002 [1962]) *Silent Spring,* which could be said to catalyze modern-day environmentalism. The catching-up process, by which women and men became similar in levels of stewardship (if less so for conservation), is really realized in cohort 4, those born within 1950–1964. Cohort 4 came of age in a period following these resurgences; they would have come of age with a religious *habitus* (few persons at that period in the U.S. were not raised in an organized religion setting) and found themselves awash in culture and institutions in which both feminism and environmentalism were "on the radar," so to speak. As I noted in chapter 4, there was a resurgence of engagement with environmental issues in the 1970s in terms of official religious doctrines (though there are many examples that predate this to draw from). Given the timetable, this is likely a *response to* bigger concerns about the reality of environmental changes. Feminism did not *drive* these changes so much as *co-creating* a broader culture in which the empowerment of women and environmental issues could be connected, or "bridged." This seems like the most plausible historical explanation given that groups such as Catholics and fundamentalist Protestants, both more likely to resist some of the trends associated with feminism, exhibit little gender difference in stewardship.

Conservation is different; I have speculated that men outpace women in conservation, *and* are more dynamic, because there is something masculine about the wilderness imaginations from which conservation sprung, historically. This imagination may have been indirectly realized within churches, through social networks, group nature outings, and the like. Caring for the environment, stewardship, and many currents of mainstream environmentalism in the mid-twentieth century may be more linked to a feminine conception of both the environment and the way in which persons are socialized. Wilderness evokes ruggedness, masculinity; conservation evokes a missive to set aside parts of the world, free from human interference—specifically *development* and *civilization*—as well as a chance to participate in something more "primal." Taken together, there is an ongoing interplay between how we are socialized to be men and women, as well as how we view and show concern for the environment, which is indirectly realized in the context of religion.

Income differences have been noted as well—religion plays less of a role among low-income persons. This is not because they don't care, but because they care more, overall. I have speculated based on research in environmental justice that this is because low-income people are more likely to bear the brunt of environmental hazards, from pollution to natural disasters—low-income people care about the environment because they *have to*. Religion plays less of a role because low-income people don't differ from one another that much by religion in their levels of environmental concern. Middle-income people have been the most dynamic in the religion–environment connection across birth cohorts, and middle-income Protestants in particular tend to have higher levels of stewardship than low- or high-income members of the same religious group. This is particularly true in younger cohorts. I have argued that this reflects the social networks in which middle-income people are more likely to grow up, participate in, and have access to. High-income people tend to have higher levels of conservation. I have argued based on the models that these are less due to religious differences than due to cultural differences, as well as priorities shaped by these cultural differences. Whereas high-income people are more likely to "pay for" stewardship in the form of regulations, taxes, and the like, high-income people can potentially "benefit from" conservation as a wilderness retreat or vacation spot. Overall, the trends from chapter 4 hold, but when it comes to income, they hold most consistently for those in the middle class.

Finally, race matters tremendously, at least among Democrats, with higher levels of conservation among Blacks than whites among Democrats for many Protestant groups. There is a "coming apart" or separation—a polarization by political party—on environmental issues that is widely evident, and likely growing. However, this divide is confined to historically white Protestant groups, and I have argued this is due to a combination of social network availability and the aging congregations of many churches within these groups. Young Republicans care more about the environment than older Republicans in the same religious group, and in general (with very few exceptions). Older people have lower stewardship levels overall, and younger people within these groups can seek out social networks containing more Republicans and Democrats with whom they can find common ground. I think it would be fair to say that, like being unaffiliated, being a Republican is something of a *master identity* (Ecklund et al. 2008, 1823), because it transcends racial differences and many religious differences as well. But the religion–environment connection isn't *really just* about party, and bringing in religion and birth cohort shows why that's the case.

So, the twin heroes of the story—*habitus* at the personal level and *reflexivity* at the level of the group—remain intact, with some complications and some growth, after these efforts to connect my work to the broader efforts of mainstream sociology, as well as try to prove myself wrong. Also, the type of motive I've tended to consider to be the most plausible—that the religion–environment concern is best understood at the "big-picture" level in terms of *indirect* or *instrumental* (Type 2) motives—seems to hold (a clear case of Type 3 motive at the personal level, as well). Environmental concern tends to either be brought into the religious sphere via external cultural and secular engagements and processes, or arises through the social networks and *habitus* of religious people. If this conclusion raises some questions for you, it also did for me. In the final chapter, I'll recap the story, look closely at some conceptual problems and other criticisms, and then fit this story into the *risk society/reflexive modernity* framework that I used in chapter 1, with some practical takeaways as far as how religion has played, and will likely continue to play, a role in how people understand, and engage with, environmental change.

Conclusion

Prospects and Possibilities

In the summer of 2015, I was working my "summer job" as a contractor, helping out my dad, repairing industrial fluid power equipment, and trying to save
money for the upcoming move. I had just finished my Master's Degree that
May and was less than a week away from moving to Kansas to pursue my
Ph.D. At the time, I lived in Fort Worth, Texas, which was being pummeled by
a severe heat wave—intense even by "August in Texas" standards. I worked
outside or in a machine shop with no air conditioning—temperatures, with the
heat index, reached over 110 degrees in the afternoon. One morning I awoke
with the worst headache I've ever had. I went to the doctor that day, who
informed me that my lungs were congested, and that I was not the first case he
had seen. He explained that it was so hot, and the air was so polluted, that a person in otherwise good physical shape needed an inhaler to get through the day.

I still have that red and gray inhaler as a reminder of that time. It wasn't a
deliberate decision to keep a memento—I'm just kind of junk collector, and
staying organized isn't my strong suit. I found it while digging through a
drawer, and I was thinking about how to phrase the conclusion of this book. It
seemed like an object from another life. As an academic, writing and teaching
from the comfort of climate-controlled indoor spaces, I sometimes wonder
how many other scholars who study environmental change have spent sum-
mers working outside in blistering heat. I also wonder how many folks who
earn a living in such heat spend think much about the human-driven environmental changes that make their jobs, and lives, more difficult and dangerous.
In both cases, surely some. My point is that the resolution that follows from
this deep dive into a world of data and modeling, theory and history, is not
purely an exercise in intellectual curiosity. I want to summarize what this
means, first, by clearly connecting the dots to describe how religion shapes
environmental concern; second, by putting this research into the context of

real-world understandings of risk, and third, by considering the role that religion and the sacred might play in the future. The second point, I am sure, has significance that extends beyond environmental change in the current context. As I complete this chapter, the death toll from the COVID-19 pandemic has surpassed 300,000 people in the U.S., after months of widespread public disagreement as to what should have been, or could be, done to prevent that number from continuing to climb. The broader context of risk leads to a series of sobering conclusions: not only can sociologists of risk offer grim insights as to why global hazards in the U.S. unfolded as they have, but also how they portend of the kinds of global hazards to come, including those associated with environmental change.

MAKING SENSE OF THE RELIGION–ENVIRONMENT CONNECTION

There are a lot of moving parts in the argument and explanation—that is, *why* the religion–environment connection is as it appears to be. For those more visually inclined, figure C.1 illustrates in greater detail what the relationships described in this book look like, based on the evidence from the models, as well as the conceptual and historical materials I drew from in order to offer explanations. I created this model based on the story arc of this work, and now, I want to say a bit more about what it means, and how it works. On the far left, I have placed *environmental change.* From the beginning of chapter 1, I argued that environmental change is something people can increasingly *witness* for themselves over time. Experts who study environmental changes

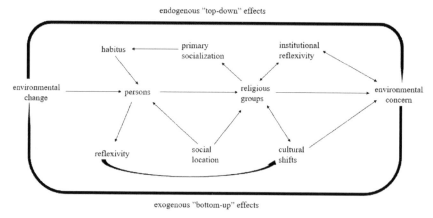

Figure C.1   The Religion–Environment Connection.

can of course test intuitions and provide additional details and information, but the impacts that human beings have had on the environment are becoming increasingly difficult to ignore. Persons *experience* environmental change. I shift from *people* to *persons* to imply in this conclusion that the experience of being human *is more than* a blob of matter simply pushed and pulled by faceless social forces, an isolated individual making decisions based on self-interest, or a voiceless hum to blend into a monotone collective. To be a *person* is to be independently purposeful, as well as *defined by* one's relationship with other persons and environment, over time (for more on *personalism,* which influences my work but does not fully define it, see Smith 2010; Stock and Szrot 2019). In figure C.1, persons are part of a *feedback loop.* As persons experience environmental change, they self-reflect (*reflexivity*). This process of self-reflection between persons leads to cultural shifts as groups of persons in ongoing dialogue begin to come to terms with change. This results in environmental concern, but also *indirectly* influences religious groups' levels of environmental concern.

Religious groups are part of the cultural landscape, and have the ability to influence culture in turn as they are increasingly brought into the loop. Religious groups, as shown here, are also *reflexive* in the sense that other institutions are—the pressures of the environment (in this case, a *cultural* environment) drive self-reflection and change. Religious groups, as shown throughout this work, respond to environmental change in a variety of ways, but they do, and have, in fact, responded, just as other institutions have had to. However, religious groups are different from other kinds of institutions because of their distinctive purchase on culture, as well as being something people are usually affected by from an early age. Not only does religion shape the moral universes of adults, but perhaps more importantly, religion is usually something people are *born into,* and begins shaping persons from an early age in ways that become "second-nature." In other words, religion as *primary socialization* is part of an *upbringing,* a *habitus,* which shapes persons in profound ways *even when those persons leave organized religion later in life.* Finally, social location—especially in terms of gender, social class, and race, as well as political party—influences both persons and religious groups, and how they come to terms with environmental change.

More broadly, the feedback loop between environmental change and environmental concern is driven by both "top-down" and "bottom-up" effects. The top-down effects are *endogenous,* which just means they come from within, and they are exerted *by* religious groups *on* persons. That is, persons learn a religious habitus from a religious group. That habitus not only shapes their views of the world and place within it, but also indirectly connects persons, from an early age, to activities, social networks, and groups that may be more likely to foster environmental concern. The "bottom-up" effects are *exogenous,* meaning they come from outside, and are exerted *by* persons, via culture, *on* religious groups. The timetable of the religion–environment connection is a multifaceted one, with a deep history, but the most widespread and explicit declarations of environmental concern among religious groups occurred between the 1970s and the 1990s, years *after* the present version of environmentalism as a culture-altering social movement arose in the U.S. A Type 2, or *indirect,* motive best, and most broadly, captures this.

Given the results of the model-building throughout this work, a direct motive (Type 1) can be safely ruled out. People who are more environmentally concerned on average tend to match those who would be expected by environmental sociologists to be more environmentally concerned anyway, closeness to one's religion is actually negatively linked to environmental concern, and the *Ex's*—those who disaffiliated—are more environmentally concerned than those who *Stay* in the religion of their upbringing. However, it is also clear that there is an *invisible* (Type 3) motive at work as well given the results in chapter 3. The *Ex's* are more environmentally concerned than those who were never religious, and this is related to the environmental concern of the religious group in which they were raised. Combined with the trends across chapters 4 and 5, religion as a source of primary socialization seems to have indirectly absorbed and transmitted some cultural dimensions of coming to terms with environmental change, particularly among those born in 1950 or later.

As environments change, human beings must either adapt to, or mitigate, present and future risks associated with environmental change (see Carmin et al. 2015; Ehrhardt-Martinez et al. 2015). This involves getting into the thorny territory of *politics.* If I'm going to "go there," I want to make sure I'm going there within the context of risk society, with a focus on the religion–environmental concern connection. In particular, Beck (1992) originally offered three possible responses to risks like the kind that environmental change poses. Rather than claiming to know what, politically, *should* be done, I focus on possibilities, including the role that religion might come to play in the context of three "risk society" scenarios—which still seem remarkably prescient decades later.

RELIGION IN RISK SOCIETY: THREE POSSIBLE VISIONS

Even if I can show that religious people have become more environmentally concerned over the past several decades, this provides only the *potential* for more widespread engagement with environmental issues. What kinds of engagements take place, what they look like, and how effective they are, will be structured in meaningful ways by the kind of society that surrounds and foregrounds them. Three broad visions are offered, lining up with the work of risk society pioneer Ulrich Beck (1992). Each represents *Die Verwandlung,* or a means by which to come to terms with the speed and scale of the environmental metamorphosis underway (see Beck 2015). The first possibility in the face of novel hazards such as those posed by human-driven environmental change can be summarized as a call to keep moving forward. As Beck (1992) notes: "The question 'what should we do?' which is asked anew by each generation, is answered by faith in progress: 'The same as ever, only bigger, faster, and more'" (224–5). This vision assumes that environmental change will be navigated, imperfectly but efficiently, by market innovations coupled with scientific and technological progress, and new hazards will be dealt with as they arise. Novel hazards, unintended side effects, crisis and instability, are expected to be addressed by the needs of "the economy," as elected representatives are increasingly expected to foster the needs of "the economy."

In this case, insofar as religion remains part of the story, it risks either being defined in exclusively negative terms or coopted by this growing techno-economic imperative. Ways of knowing framed as *religious* or *spiritual,* and thereby existing outside these market- and progress-driven logics, would likely become construed as obstacles to progress. A version of progress defined in technological and economic terms may push religious groups further into a defensive posture, throttling their ability to make meaningful cultural impacts or moral progress on issues such as environmental change. However, the biggest problem that faces a commitment to this first scenario is that policy changes, as Beck (1992) notes, will always have "winners and losers, from risks" (227). This is the case whether the debate is about what should and shouldn't be taught in public schools, who should have access to abortion or contraception and when, what employees and businesses are considered *essential* during a pandemic—or who will benefit from, and who will pay for, efforts to mitigate or adapt to environmental change. Market logics, wedded to technical innovation, take for granted that some will benefit. It is less often acknowledged that these benefits are *relational*—such benefits often occur at the expense of others (Curran 2018), anticipating a technological society structured around power itself as a singular virtue (see Stivers 1999).

Environmental concern, as I have found here, is not directly in opposition to the cultural values of religious groups overall. Even sectarian, fundamentalist Protestant groups have increased in levels of both stewardship and conservation, and there is not a consistent divide by cultural orientation, with liberals taking one side and fundamentalists, another. However, in the context of this first scenario, environmental concern arising indirectly from religious group identity can be expected to come into conflict with other political priorities or economic concerns. That the U.S. has tended to go this route has amplified difficulties in translating relatively high levels of environmental concern into more consistent environmental action. It is also a major factor in growing polarization and resentment across social class, party, and racial/ ethnic lines, which further complicates future engagement at the intersection of religion and the environment. Perhaps most evident in the current crisis, a high-stakes socio-cultural field which presumes winners and losers, coupled with a singular emphasis on technical and economic efficiency, leads to wide-spread resentment and erosion of social trust, leading to unrest and extremism (see Szrot 2020b). That COVID-19 has revealed broad, deep, and numerous political, economic, social, and cultural fault lines in the U.S. is clear. These fault lines will not simply go away, but left unaddressed, will likely only be amplified by future global hazards. This approach to global hazards is being tested. It may or may not hold, but it currently groans under the strain.

The second possibility is that hazards might be addressed within the context of an expanded welfare state. In this, environmental change can be slowed or even reversed through ongoing regulatory efforts and state reform, including expanded bureaucratic and public science enterprises (Beck 1992, 228–31). In the second scenario, religion may fare worse. The reason for this is connected to the existential security theory (see Norris and Inglehart 2011): wealthy countries with strong safety nets tend to see populations gradually withdrawing from organized religion, as is the case among many countries in Western Europe at present. The welfare state can be expected to provide health, wealth, education, and more, and there are undoubtedly material benefits to this approach.

There is, however, a growth in bureaucracy, and greater empowerment of a specific kind of scientific expertise, most comfortable operating in this context. The potential dangers of bureaucratic growth have been chronicled at least since founding sociologist Max Weber (1946) pointed out both their durability and undemocratic tendencies (228–44). Bureaucracy, once established, is quite difficult to remove, or even *move,* even if it becomes repressive or dysfunctional. The empowerment of scientific expertise that should drive, and be driven, by the welfare state has not translated to higher levels of scientific confidence in Western Europe. In fact, Norris and Inglehart (2011) found a modest *positive* relationship between confidence in scientific advances and religiosity of a country (68). Perhaps, then, there is something that religion provides, which is compatible with the scientific enterprise, but cannot be supplanted by expansion of state bureaucracy and scientific expertise. Whether this approach fares better, or is sustainable, is an open question. However, dangers inhere of reasserted and empowered technical expertise, couched in expansive bureaucratic machinery, leading away from greater human freedom and more qualitative dimensions of flourishing.

A third vision involves "de-centering" politics, such that a greater degree of critical self-reflection is possible within all institutions. This begins to look more like a call for *more democracy,* or at least, for a democracy populated by people and institutions that are necessarily more *reflexive* (Beck 1992, 231–5). This vision of *reflexive modernity* involves society as a whole and its institutions becoming more self-reflective in the face of present and possible future hazards. Beck's initial vision, like many grand sociological perspectives dating back to the nineteenth century, presumes secularization. However, I have argued that, though there are places and times in which persons might become less religious on average, there are good reasons to suspect that religion is not going away anytime soon, despite ongoing pronouncements about living in a secular age. I have shown with data that religion is reflexive, indicating varied and uneven increases in environmental concern occurring alongside environmental change. But what specifically happens *within* religious groups that can foster a virtuous interplay of science and democracy, such that science becomes more democratized, and democratic peoples, more reflexive? One possibility, offered by sociologist Daniel Bell (1996) in his work *The Cultural Contradictions of Capitalism*: "What religion can restore is the continuity of generations, returning us to the existential predicaments which are the ground of humility and care for others. Yet such a continuity cannot be manufactured, nor a cultural revolution engineered. That thread woven out of those experiences which give one a tragic sense of life, a life that is lived on the knife-edge of finitude and freedom" (30).

This continuity is not to be found in a stimulus-response, religious-congruence model of human behavior, in which religious persons are told by religious leaders, sacred texts, or doctrine what to do, and then they do it. Religion, like all things human beings do together, is a complex phenomenon, full of incongruity and flux. Humility, care for others, and a sense of the tragic do not lead directly to *progress* along economic or technical lines, but may instead provide an ongoing, constructive, and authentically human-affirming criticism of it. In asking "Does democracy deserve to survive?" historian and cultural critic Christopher Lasch argues that religion provides a check on extremism—such as through the consistent condemnation of idolatry to be found in the Judeo-Christian tradition (1996, 90). Neither set of ideas represents an effort to chip away at the wall of separation between church and state, nor undermine the ongoing quest for greater knowledge and insight. Both sets of ideas invite and affirm self-reflection, as well as offering a standpoint from which to get some critical distance from a potentially burgeoning new "religion" of techno-economic progress.

The third dimension along which religion can foster reflexivity simply involves the fact that religious groups are able to form a kind of community, an ongoing reinforcement of norms and social bonds that can serve in a local way to strengthen the fabric of a more expansive democracy. Not only is there evidence that churches and other religious settings can provide a real-world opportunity for deliberation about difficult issues (Neilheisel 2009), but also religious institutions can provide a means by which to access a broader array of *social capital* including social networks and voluntary institutions. These networks not only have many personal benefits, but also are the bulwark of trust between persons and bigger political and economic factors (see Putnam 2000). A society without spaces through which these activities take place might become more divided, losing trust in its institutions and perhaps in the democratic processes or rule of law. There are worrying trends in this direction at present in the U.S. And on that note, if I'm going to call for more and better self-reflection, I'd better lead by example.

CODA: REFLEXIVITY, RELIGION, AND SCIENCE

I suspect that deeply religious persons might be suspicious of my arguments for implicitly assuming that religions *should be* more environmentally concerned according to the ways environmental concern is measured here. I might even be accused of shoehorning some kind of New Age spirituality into long-standing religious traditions. To be clear, my primary goal has been to *describe* trends in environmental concern among religious groups, not to lecture religious people on what they should be doing. However, it would be in bad faith not to state that I see higher levels of environmental concern as a good thing, and cause for hope. Surely years of research are an investment that betrays one's own views and interests in terms of what is both important and worthy of attention. I am deeply concerned about the environment, and that the means by which the U.S. and the world are thus far addressing environmental change is insufficient to the scale and potential consequences of it.

On the other hand, avowedly secular persons might reach the end of this book and say: but surely other institutions can do the things that religion is doing in this story, and perhaps do them better, right? It has been bemoaned by many secular thinkers that it's really difficult to organize secular persons around their secularity. In his in-depth research into secularity, sociologist Phil Zuckerman (2014) found great variation in secularity. There are those who are spiritual, holding spiritual beliefs but not members of organized religious groups; there is a large population of "soft secularists" who are not religious but tend to have a conciliatory view of religion; there are those who are apathetic about being secular, and give it little thought. There are also, however, secularists who are quite "religious" in their secularity, and spend a great deal of time organizing secular community and engaging in broader cultural and political efforts. Many secular people are simply not "joiners" and do not feel a want or need to organize around their secularity. And if they did, would there quickly be a veritable smorgasbord of secular institutions, much as is the case with religious ones? The question of what it means to be "religious" or "secular" would need to be visited anew. Whether, and to what extent, this happens in the future is also an open question.

These anticipated objections raise an old set of questions about the role and relationship between religion and science. Such a debate is far-reaching and philosophically profound. My aim here, as in many other matters, is more narrowly practical. I am reminded of the words of biologist and conservationist Edward O. Wilson (2006), who speaks as a secular scientist to an imagined Bible-believing interlocutor:

> For you, the glory of an unseen divinity; for me, the glory of the universe revealed at last. For you, the belief in God made flesh to save mankind; for me, the belief in Promethean fire seized to set men free. You have found your final truth; I am still searching. I may be wrong, you may be wrong. We may both be partly right. Does this difference in worldview separate us in all things? It does not. You and I and every other human being strive for the same imperatives of security, freedom of choice, personal dignity, and a cause to believe in that is larger than ourselves. Let us see, then, if we can, and if you are willing, to meet on the near side of metaphysics in order to deal with the real world we share. I put it this way because you have the power to solve a great problem about which I care deeply. I suggest we set aside our differences in order to save the Creation...religion and science are the two most powerful forces in the world today, including especially the United States. If religion and science could be united on the common ground of biological conservation, the problem would soon be solved (4–5).

To meet on the near side of metaphysics is far simpler to say than to do. As much time as I spend studying the social world and its importance, I am not a joiner. And years of studying philosophy and religion have not offered me some special guidance or privileged standpoint from which to do this, though I hold with Wilson that it can be done. As much time as I spend in solitude, reading, writing, and crunching numbers, I uphold the hope that such efforts must be inherently deliberative, social, imperfect, ongoing. Studying the social world often means taking a step back, making sense of what is counterintuitive, as well as making intuitive sense of findings based on experience, though it may have long remained filtered from direct perception.

Sociology connects art to science, philosophy and mathematics to empathy and emotion, providing hope of translating what is profound, and reconciling seemingly insurmountable divides. Like many sociologists, I hope that my work might contribute in some small way to improving the world and benefiting those who live in it, but the passions that drive it are rooted in a curiosity informed by personal struggles and circumstances. I was raised Catholic and working-class, developed a passion for scientific knowledge, left the church without being confirmed at age 16, spent several years studying religion from a philosophical angle, became an atheist, faced some personal difficulties in my late twenties, reconsidered faith, and remained deeply interested in the existential questions raised by my life experiences and time spent studying religion. But this story started long before that. I was a kid who liked spending time outside, an active Scout and amateur outdoor explorer, long concerned about the environment and the future. The scholarly passion was rekindled by the 2015 papal Encyclical letter *Laudato si'* by Pope Francis; the personal emotion has been driven by watching environmental change unfold before my eyes over the decades, sometimes with tragic consequences. The drive has been nurtured and motivated by friends and family, by mentors and fellow sociologists, and by a concern about the future of both the environment and democracy in the U.S. and beyond. It is not the end, nor a beginning, but a modest contribution to a much longer story, about how human beings address problems, build relationships, and make sense of their place in the cosmos.

References

Antonio, Robert J. 2009. "Climate Change, the Resource Crunch, and the Global Growth Imperative." In *Current Perspectives in Social Theory*, Volume 26, edited by H.F. Dahms, 3–73. Bingley: Emerald.

Antonio, Robert J. and Robert J. Brulle. 2011. "The Unbearable Lightness of Politics: Climate Change Denial and Political Polarization." *The Sociological Quarterly* 52: 195–202.

Baggett, Jerome P. 2019. *The Varieties of Nonreligious Experience: Atheism in American Culture*. New York: New York University Press.

Balint, Peter J., Ronald E. Stewart, Anand Desai and Lawrence C. Waters. 2011. *Wicked Environmental Problems: Managing Uncertainty and Conflict*. Washington, DC: Island Press.

Barnosky, Anthony D. 2008. "Megafauna Biomass Tradeoff as a Driver of Quaternary and Future Extinctions." *PNAS* 105, no. 1: 11543–8.

Barry, Carolyn McNamara and Mona M. Abo-Zena, eds. 2014. *Emerging Adults' Religiousness and Spirituality: Meaning-Making in an Age of Transition*. New York: Oxford University Press.

BBC. 2019. "Paris Climate Accords: US Notifies UN of Intention to Withdraw." *BBC News, United States & Canada*, September 4, 2019. https://www.bbc.com/news/world-us-canada-50297029

Beck, Ulrich. 1992. *Risk Society: Towards a New Modernity*. Thousand, Oaks: Sage.

Beck, Ulrich. 2015. "Emancipatory Catastrophism: What Does It Mean to Climate Change and Risk Society." *Current Sociology*, 63, no. 1: 75–88.

Bell, Daniel. 1996. *The Cultural Contradictions of Capitalism*. New York: Basic Books.

Bellah, Robert N., Richard Madsen, William M. Sullivan, Ann Swidler and Steven M. Tipton. 1996. *Habits of the Heart: Individualism and Commitment in American Life*. Berkeley: University of California Press.

Berger, Peter L. 1967. *The Sacred Canopy*. New York: Doubleday.

Berry, Evan. 2015. *Devoted to Nature: The Religious Roots of American Environmentalism*. Oakland: University of California Press.

Bourdieu, Pierre. 1986. "The Forms of Capital." In *Handbook of Theory and Research for the Sociology of Education*, edited by J. Richardson, 241–58. Westport: Greenwood.

Bourdieu, Pierre. 1993. *The Field of Cultural Production*. Edited and Introduced by Randal Johnson. Columbia: Columbia University Press.

Bourdieu, Pierre. 2002. *Distinction: A Social Critique of the Judgement of Taste*. Translated by Richard Nice. Cambridge: Harvard University Press.

Brulle, Robert J. and Robert J. Antonio. 2015. "The Pope's Fateful Vision of Hope for Society and the Planet." *Nature Climate Change* 5, no. 10: 900–1. https://doi.org/10.1038/nclimate2796

Bullard, Robert Doyle. 1994. *Unequal Protection: Environmental Justice and Communities of Color*. San Francisco: Sierra Club Books.

Bullard, Robert and Beverly Hendrix Wright 1987. "Environmentalism and the Politics of Equity: Emergent Trends in the Black Community." *Mid-American Review of Sociology* 12, no. 2: 21–37.

Buttel, Frederick H. 1979. "Age and Environmental Concern: A Multivariate Analysis." *Youth & Society* 10 (March): 237–56.

Buttel, Frederick H. 2004. "The Treadmill of Production: An Appreciation, Assessment, and Agenda for Research." *Organization & Environment* 17, no. 3: 323–36.

Campbell, Joseph. 1986. *The Inner Reaches of Outer Space: Metaphor as Myth and as Religion*. New York: Harper & Row Publishers, Inc.

Carlisle, Juliet E. and April K. Clark. 2018. "Green for God: Religion and Environmentalism by Cohort and Time." *Environment and Behavior* 50, no. 2: 213–41.

Carson, Rachel. 2002 [1962]. *Silent Spring: 40th Anniversary Edition*. Boston: Mariner Books.

Carvalho, Anabela. 2015. "The Pope's Encyclical as a Call for Democratic Climate Change." *Nature Climate Change* 5, no. 10: 905–7. https://doi.org/10.1038/nclimate2799

Chakraborty, Jayajit, Timothy W. Collins and Sara E. Grineski. 2019. "Exploring the Environmental Justice Implications of Hurricane Harvey Flooding in Greater Houston, Texas." *American Journal of Public Health* 109, no. 2: 244–50.

Chaves, Mark. 2010. "Rain Dances in the Dry Season: Overcoming the Religious Congruence Fallacy." *Journal for the Scientific Study of Religion* 49, no. 1: 1–14.

Chaves, Mark. 2017. *American Religion: Contemporary Trends*. Princeton: Princeton University Press.

Chavis, Benjamin F. and Charles Lee. 1987. *Toxic Wastes and Race in the United States*. New York: United Church of Christ.

Christoff, Peter and Robyn Eckersley. 2013. *Globalization and the Environment*. Lanham: Rowman & Littlefield Publishers, Inc.

Clements, John M., Aaron M. McCright and Chenyang Xiao. 2014. "Green Christians? An Empirical Examination of Environmental Concern within the U.S. General Public." *Organization & Environment* 27, no. 1: 85–102.

Cox, Harvey. 1966. *The Secular City*. New York: The Macmillan Company.

Crutzen, Paul. 2002. "The Geography of Mankind." *Nature* 415: 23. https://doi.org/10.1038/415023a

Curran, Dean 2017. "The Treadmill of Production and the Positional Economy of Consumption." *Canadian Review of Sociology* 54, no. 1: 29–47.

Curran, Dean. 2018. "Environmental Justice Meets Risk-Class: The Relational Distribution of Environmental *Bads*." *Antipode* 50, no. 2: 298–318.

Daly, Herman E. 1996. *Beyond Growth: The Economics of Sustainable Development*. Boston: Beacon Press.

Danielsen, Sabrina. 2013. "Fracturing Over Creation Care? Shifting Environmental Beliefs among Evangelicals, 1984–2010." *Journal for the Scientific Study of Religion* 52, no. 1: 198–215.

Davies, Paul. 1983. *God and the New Physics*. New York: Simon and Schuster.

Djupe, Paul A. and Patrick Kieran Hunt. 2009. "Beyond the Lynn White Thesis: Congregational Effects on Environmental Concern." *Journal for the Scientific Study of Religion* 48, no. 4: 670–86.

Dunlap, Riley E. and Robert E. Jones. 2002. "Environmental Concern: Conception and Measurement Issues." In *Handbook of Environmental Sociology*, edited by Riley E. Dunlap and William Michelson, 482–524. Westport: Greenwood Press.

Dunlap, Riley E. and Aaron M. McCright. 2015. "Challenging Climate Change: The Denial Countermovement." In *Climate Change and Society: Sociological Perspectives*, edited by Riley E. Dunlap and Robert J. Brulle, 300–32. New York: Oxford University Press.

Eckberg, Douglas Lee and T. Jean Blocker. 1989. "Varieties of Religious Involvement and Environmental Concern: Testing the Lynn White Thesis." *Journal for the Scientific Study of Religion* 28, no. 4: 509–17.

Eckberg, Douglas Lee and T. Jean Blocker. 1996. "Christianity, Environmentalism, and the Theoretical Problem of Fundamentalism." *Journal for the Scientific Study of Religion* 35, no. 4: 343–55.

Ecklund, Elaine and Jerry Z. Park. 2009. "Conflict Between religion and Science among Academic Scientists?" *Journal for the Scientific Study of Religion* 48, no. 2: 276–92.

Ecklund, Elaine and Christopher P. Scheitle. 2007. "Religion among Academic Scientists: Distinctions, Disciplines, and Demographics." *Social Problems* 54, no. 2: 289–307.

Ecklund, Elaine, David R. Johnson, Brandon Vaidyanathan, Kirstin R.W. Matthews, Steven W. Lewis, Robert A. Thomson Jr., Di Di. 2019. *Secularity and Science: What Scientists around the World Really Think about Religion*. New York: Oxford University Press.

Edenhofer, Ottmar, Christian Flachsland and Brigitte Knopf. 2015. "Science and Religion in Dialogue over the Global Commons." *Nature Climate Change* 5, no. 10: 907–9. https://doi.org/10.1038/nclimate2798

Ehrlich, Paul and John Harte. 2015. "Biophysical Limits, Women's Rights and the Climate Encyclical." *Nature Climate Change* 5, no. 10: 904–5. https://doi.org/10.1038/nclimate2795

Ellingson, Stephen. 2016. *To Care for Creation: The Emergence of the Religious Environmental Movement.* Chicago: The University of Chicago Press.

Emerson, Michael O. and Christian Smith. 2000. *Divided by Faith: Evangelical Religion and the Problem of Race in America.* New York: Oxford University Press.

Ergas, Christina and Richard York. 2012. "Women's Status and Carbon Dioxide Emissions: A Quantitative Cross-National Analysis." *Social Science Research* 41: 965–76.

Evans, John H. 2013. "The Growing Social and Moral Conflict between Conservative Protestantism and Science." *Journal for the Scientific Study of Religion* 52, no. 2: 368–85.

Eve, Raymond A. and Francis B. Harrold. 1990. *The Creationist Movement in Modern America.* Boston: Twayne Publishers.

Farrell, Justin. 2015. *The Battle for Yellowstone: Morality and the Sacred Roots of Environmental Conflict.* Princeton: Princeton University Press.

Finke, Roger and Rodney Stark. 2007. *The Churching of America 1776–2005: Winners and Losers in Our Religious Economy.* New Brunswick: Rutgers University Press

Fisher, James T. 2000. *Catholics in the United States.* New York: Oxford University.

Foster, John Bellamy. 1999. "Marx's Theory of Metabolic Rift: Classical Foundations for Environmental Sociology 1." *American Journal of Sociology* 105, no. 2: 366–405.

Francis. 2015. *Encyclical Letter Laudato si, On the Care for Our Common Home.* May 24, 2015. http://w2.vatican.va/content/francesco/en/encyclicals/documents/papa-francesco_20150524_enciclica-laudato-si.html

Friedan, Betty. 1963. *The Feminine Mystique.* New York: Norton.

Gauchat, Gordon. 2012. "Politicization of Science in the Public Sphere: A Study of Public Trust in the United States, 1974 to 2010." *American Sociological Review* 77, no. 2:167–87.

Gerten, Dieter, Martin Schönfeld and Bernhard Schauberger. 2018. "On Deeper Human Dimensions in Earth System Analysis and Modeling." *Earth System Dynamics* 9: 849–63.

Giddens, Anthony. 1990. *The Consequences of Modernity.* Stanford: Stanford University Press.

Giddens, Anthony. 2000. *Runaway World: How Globalization is Reshaping Our Lives.* New York: Routledge.

Gottlieb, Roger S. 1996. *This Sacred Earth: Religion, Nature, Environment.* New York: Routledge.

Gould, Stephen Jay. 2011. *The Hedgehog, the Fox, and the Magister's Pox: Mending the Gap between Science and the Humanities.* Cambridge: The Belknap Press of Harvard University Press.

Grim, John and Mary Evelyn Tucker. 2015. *Ecology and Religion.* Washington, DC: Island Press.

Gross, Neil and Solon Simmons. 2009. "The Religiosity of American College and University Professors." *Sociology of Religion* 70, no. 2: 101–29.

Guth, James L., John C. Green, Lyman A. Kellstedt and Corwin E. Smidt. 1995. "Faith and the Environment: Religious Beliefs and Attitudes on Environmental Policy." *American Journal of Political Science* 39, no. 2: 364–82.

Hale, Christopher J. 2015. "Jeb Bush's Response to Pope Francis's Climate Change Encyclical is Hogwash." *Time*, June 17, 2015. https://www.google.com/amp/amp .timeinc.net/ime/3924287/pope-francis-climate-change/%3fsource=dam

Halton, Eugene. 2019. "John Stuart-Glennie's Lost Legacy." In *Forgotten Founders and Other Neglected Theorists*, edited by Christopher T. Conner, Nicholas M. Baxter and David R. Dickens, 11–26. Lanham: Lexington Books.

Hamilton, Clive. 2013. *Earth Masters: The Dawn of the Age of Climate Engineering*. New Haven: Yale University Press.

Hamlin, Christopher and David M. Lodge. 2006. "Beyond Lynn White: Religion, the Context of Ecology, and the Flux of Nature." In *Religion and the New Ecology*, edited by Lodge, David M. and Christopher Hamlin, 1–25. Notre Dame: University of Notre Dame Press.

Hand, Carl M. and Kent D. Van Liere. 1984. "Religion, Mastery-Over-Nature, and Environmental Concern." *Social Forces* 63, no. 2: 555–70.

Harlan, Sharon L., David N. Pellow and J. Timmons Roberts, Shannon Elizabeth Bell, William G. Holt and Joane Nagel. 2015. "Climate Justice and Inequality." In *Climate Change and Society: Sociological Perspectives*, edited by Dunlap, Riley E. and Robert J. Brulle, 127–63. New York: Oxford University Press.

Harvey, David. 1990. *The Condition of Postmodernity: An Enquiry into the Origins of Cultural Change*. Cambridge: Blackwell.

Hayhoe, Katherine and Andrew Farley. 2011. *A Climate for Change: Global Warming Facts for Faith-Based Decisions*. New York: FaithWords.

Hellevik, Ottar. 2009. "Linear versus Logistic Regression when the Dependent Variable is a Dichotomy." *Qualitative Quantitative* 43: 59–74.

Hoffman, John. 2004. *Generalized Linear Models: An Applied Approach*. Boston: Allyn & Bacon, Inc.

Hoffman, Lesa. 2015. *Longitudinal Analysis: Modeling Within-Person Fluctuation and Change*. New York: Routledge.

Holmes, Jack. 2017. "There Is Now One Nation on Planet Earth That Has Not Signed on to the Paris Climate Accords." *Esquire*, November 7, 2017. http:// www.esquire.com/news-politics/a13444828/syria-paris-climate-accords-united -states/

Hunter, James Davison. 1991. *Culture Wars: The Struggle to Define America*. New York: Basic Books.

Iannaccone, Lawrence R. 1994. "Why Strict Churches are Strong." *American Journal of Sociology* 99, no. 5: 1180–211.

Ishihara, Hiroe. 2018. "Relational Values from a Cultural Valuation Perspective: How Can Sociology Contribute to the Evaluation of Ecosystem Services?" *Current Opinion in Environmental Sustainability* 35: 61–8.

Jameson, Fredric. 1984. "Postmodernism, or the Logic of Late Capitalism," *New Left Review* 146 (July/August): 53–92.

Jenkins, Richard. 1992. *Pierre Bourdieu*. London: Routledge.

Jenkins, Willis. 2018. "'The Mysterious Silence of Mother Earth in *Laudato si'*.'" *Journal of Religious Ethics* 46, no. 3: 441–62.

John XXIII. 1961. *Mater et Magistra*. May 15, 2017. http://www.vatican.va/content/john-xxiii/fr/encyclicals/documents/hf_j-xxiii_enc_15051961_mater.html

John Paul II. 1979. *Bula Inter Sanctos Proclaiming Saint Francis of Assisi as Patron of Ecology*. November 29, 1979. http://francis35.org/english/papal-declaration-francis-patron-ecology/

John Paul II. 1987. *Meeting with the Native Peoples of the Americas*. September 14, 1987. http://w2.vatican.va/content/john-paul-ii/en/speeches/1987/september/documents/hf_jp_ii_spe_19870914_amerindi-phoenix.html

Jones, Robert P. 2016. *The End of White Christian America*. New York: Simon & Schuster.

Kanagy, Conrad L. and Hart M. Nelsen. 1995. "Religion and Environmental Concern: Challenging the Dominant Assumptions." *Review of Religious Research* 37, no. 1: 33–45.

Kasper, Debbie V.S. 2009. "Ecological Habitus: Toward a Better Understanding of Socioecological Relations." *Organization & Environment* 22, no. 3: 311–26.

Kirby, Jeff. 2020. "Fleshing Out an Ecological Habitus: Field and Capitals of Radical Environmental Movements." *Nature and Culture* 12, no. 2: 89–114.

Klein, Naomi. 2014. *This Changes Everything: Capitalism versus the Climate*. New York: Simon & Schuster.

Kolbert, Elizabeth. 2014. *The Sixth Extinction: An Unnatural History*. New York: Henry Holt and Company.

Konisky, David M. 2018. "The Greening of Christianity? A Study of Environmental Attitudes over Time." *Environmental Politics* 27: 267–91.

Land, Richard C. and Louis A. Moore. 1992. *The Earth is the Lord's: Christians and the Environment*. Nashville: Southern Baptist Convention Sunday School Board.

Lasch, Christopher. 1995. *The Revolt of the Elites and the Betrayal of Democracy*. New York: W.W. Norton & Company.

Lemert, Charles. 2012. *Social Things: An Introduction to the Social Life*. 5th edition. Lanham, MD: Rowman & Littlefield Publishers, Inc.

Lenzer, Gertrud, ed. 1998. *Auguste Comte and Positivism*. New Brunswick: Transaction Publishers.

Lidskog, Rolf, Arthur PJ Mol and Peter Oosterveer. 2015. "Towards a Global Environmental Sociology? Legacies, Trends and Future Directions." *Current Sociology* 63, no. 3: 339–68.

Long, David E. 2011. *Evolution and Religion in American Education*. New York: Springer.

Lyotard, Jean-Francois. 1985. *The Post-Modern Condition*. Minneapolis: University of Minnesota Press.

Mannheim, Karl. 1952. "The Problem of Generations." In *Essays on the Sociology of Knowledge*, edited by P. Kecskemeti, 276–322. New York: Oxford University Press.

Masci, David. 2014. "The Divide over Ordaining Women." *Pew Research Center*, September 9, 2014. https://www.pewresearch.org/fact-tank/2014/09/09/the-divide-over-ordaining-women/

McCright, Aaron and Chenyang Xiao. 2014. "Gender and Environmental Concern: Insights from Recent Work and Future Research." *Society & Natural Resources* 27, no. 10: 1109–13.

McDonald, Yolanda and Nicole E. Jones. "Drinking Water Violations and Environmental Justice in the United States, 2011–2015." *American Journal of Public Health* 108, no. 10: 1401–7.

Meyer, Robinson. 2017. "Did Donald Trump Just Make the Planet Hotter?" *The Atlantic*, June 1, 2017. https://www.google.com/amp/s/www.theatlantic.com/amp/article/525222/

Mohai, Paul and Robin Saha. 2006. "Reassessing Racial and Socioeconomic Disparities in Environmental Justice Research." *Demography* 43, no. 2: 383–99.

Mohai, Paul and Robin Saha. 2007. "Racial Inequality in the Distribution of Hazardous Waste: A National-Level Reassessment." *Social Problems* 54, no. 3: 343–70.

Mohai, Paul and Ben W. Twight. 1987. "Age and Environmentalism: An Elaboration of the Buttel Model Using National Survey Evidence." *Social Science Quarterly* 68, no. 4:798–815.

Mohai, Paul, David Pellow and J. Timmons Roberts. 2009. "Environmental Justice." *Annual Review of Environment and Resources* 34: 405–30.

Mood, Carina. 2010. "Logistic Regression: Why We Cannot Do What We Think We Can Do, and What We Can Do About It." *European Sociological Review* 26, no. 1: 67–82.

Mooney, Chris. 2005. *The Republican War on Science*. New York: Basic Books.

Nash, Roderick. 1996. "The Greening of Religion." In *This Sacred Earth: Religion, Nature, Environment*, edited by Roger S. Gottlieb, 194–229. New York: Routledge.

Neilheisel, Jacob R. 2009. "Veni, Vidi, Disseri: Churches and the Promise of Democratic Deliberation." *American Politics Research* 37, no. 4: 614–43.

Norris, Pippa and Ronald Inglehart. 2011. *Sacred and Secular: Religion and Politics Worldwide*. New York: Cambridge University Press.

Oreskes, Naomi and Erik M. Conway. 2010. *Merchants of Doubt: How a Handful of Scientists Obscured the Truth on Everything from Tobacco Smoke to Global Warming*. New York: Bloomsbury Press.

Palmeri, Frank. 2016. *State of Nature, Stages of Society: Enlightenment Conjectural History and Modern Social Discourse*. New York: Columbia University Press.

Pampel, Fred C. and Lori M. Hunter. 2012. "Cohort Change, Diffusion, and Support for Environmental Spending in the United States." *American Journal of Sociology* 118, no. 2: 420–48.

Pearce, Lisa D. and Melinda Lundquist Denton. 2011. *A Faith of Their Own: Stability and Change in the Religiosity of America's Adolescents*. New York: Oxford University Press.

Pew Research Center. 2014. *How Americans Feel about Religious Groups*. July 16, 2014. https://www.pewforum.org/2014/07/16/how-americans-feel-about-religious-groups/

Pinker, Steven. 2011. *The Better Angels of Our Nature: Why Violence Has Declined*. New York: Penguin Books.

Pinker, Steven. 2016. *The Blank Slate: The Modern Denial of Human Nature.* New York: Penguin Books.

Pogue, Neall W. 2016. *The Lost Environmentalists: The Struggle between Conservative Protestants and the Environmental Movement.* PhD diss., Texas A&M University.

Polletta, Francesca. 2008. "Culture and Movements." *The ANNALS of the American Academy of Political and Social Science* 619 (September):78–96.

Popper, Karl. 1962. *Conjectures and Refutations.* London: Routledge.

Public Religion Research Institute. 2012. *The 2012 American Values Survey.* http://publicreligion.org/site/wp-content/uploads/2012/10/AVS-2012-Pre-election-Report-for-Web.pdf

Purdy, Jedediah. 2015. *After Nature: A Politics for the Anthropocene.* Cambridge: Harvard University Press.

Putnam, Robert D. 2000. *Bowling Alone: The Collapse and Revival of American Community.* New York: Simon & Schuster.

Raven, Peter H. 2016. "Our World and Pope Francis' Encyclical, *Laudato si.*" *The Quarterly Review of Biology* 91, no. 3: 247–60.

Regnerus, Mark. 2007. *Forbidden Fruit: Sex & Religion in the Lives of American Teenagers.* New York: Oxford University Press.

Rittel, Horst W.J. and Melvin M. Webber. 1973. "Dilemmas in a General Theory of Planning." *Policy Sciences* 4, no. 2: 155–69.

Roof, Wade Clark and William McKinney. 1992. *American Mainline Religion: Its Changing Shape and Future.* New Brunswick: Rutgers University Press.

Rothstein, Richard. 2017. *The Color of Law: A Forgotten History of How Our Government Segregated America.* New York: Liveright.

Rosa, Eugene A., Thomas K. Rudel, Richard York, Andrew K. Jorgenson and Thomas Dietz. 2015. "The Human (Anthropogenic) Driving Forces of Climate Change." *Climate Change and Society: Sociological Perspectives,* edited by Riley E. Dunlap and Robert J. Brulle, 32–60. New York: Oxford University Press.

Ruddiman, William F. 2003. "The Anthropogenic Greenhouse Era began Thousands of Years Ago." *Climactic Change* 61: 261–93.

Ruddiman, William F., Erle C. Ellis, Jed O. Kaplan and Dorian Q. Fuller. 2015. "Defining the Epoch We Live In: Is a Formally Designated 'Anthropocene' a Good Idea?" *Science* 348 (6230): 38–9.

Saha, Robin and Paul Mohai. 2005. "Historical Context and Hazardous Waste Facility Siting: Understanding Temporal Patterns in Michigan." *Social Problems* 52, no. 4: 618–48.

Sawyer, Suzana. 2004. *Crude Chronicles: Indigenous Politics, Multinational Oil, and Neoliberalism in Ecuador.* Durham: Duke University Press.

Scheitle, Christopher P. 2011. "Religious and Spiritual Change in College: Assessing the Effect of a Science Education." *Sociology of Education* 84, no. 2: 122–36.

Schut, Russell, Rengin Firat and David Sloan Wilson. 2020. "Debate: Nothing in Sociology Makes Sense Except in the Light of Evolution." *This View of Life* Special Issue https://thisviewoflife.com/debate-nothing-in-sociology-makes-sense-except-in-the-light-of-evolution/

Schwadel, Philip and Erik Johnson. 2017. "The Religious and Political Origins of Evangelical Protestants' Opposition to Environmental Spending." *Journal for the Scientific Study of Religion* 56, no. 1: 179–98.

Shaiko, Ronald G. 1987. "Religion, Politics, and Environmental Concern: A Powerful Mix of Passions." *Social Science Quarterly* 68, no. 2: 244–62.

Shelton, Jason E. and Michael O. Emerson. 2012. *Blacks and Whites in Christian America: How Racial Discrimination Shapes Religious Convictions*. New York: New York University Press.

Shepherd, Nicholas M. 2010. "Religious Socialization and a Reflexive Habitus: Christian Youth Groups as Sites for Identity Work." In *Religion and Youth*, edited by Sylvia Collins-Mayo and Pink Dandelion, 147–55. London: Ashgate.

Sherkat, Darren E. and Christopher G. Ellison. 2007. "Structuring the Religion-Environment Connection: Identifying Religious Influences on Environmental Concern and Activism." *Journal for the Scientific Study of Religion* 46, no. 1: 71–85.

Shermer, Michael. 2003. *How We Believe: Science, Skepticism, and the Search for God*. New York: Henry Holt and Company.

Smith, Angela M. and Simone Pulver. 2009. "Ethics-Based Environmentalism in Practice: Religious-Environmental Organizations in the United States." *Worldviews* 13: 145–79.

Smith, Christian. 2010. *What is a Person? Rethinking Humanity, Social Life, and the Moral Good from the Person Up*. Chicago: University of Chicago Press.

Smith, Christian. 2014. *The Sacred Project of American Sociology*. New York: Oxford University Press.

Smith, Christian and Melinda Lundquist Denton. 2005. *Soul Searching: The Religious and Spiritual Lives of American Teenagers*. New York: Oxford University Press.

Smith, Christian and Patricia Snell. 2009. *Souls in Transition: The Religious and Spiritual Lives of Emerging Adults*. New York: Oxford.

Smith, Tom W. 1990. "Classifying Protestant Denominations." *Review of Religious Research* 31, no. 3: 225–45.

Smith, Tom W., Peter Marsden, Michael Hout and Jibum Kim. *General Social Surveys, 1972–2014* [machine-readable data file] /Principal Investigator, Tom W. Smith; Co-Principal Investigator, Peter V. Marsden; Co-Principal Investigator, Michael Hout; Sponsored by National Science Foundation.—NORC ed.—Chicago: NORC at the University of Chicago [producer]; Storrs, CT: The Roper Center for Public Opinion Research, University of Connecticut [distributor], 2015.

Steensland, Brian, Jerry Z. Park, Mark D. Regnerus, Lynn D. Robinson, W. Bradford Wilcox and Robert D. Woodberry. 2000. "The Measure of American Religion: Toward Improving the State of the Art." *Social Forces* 79, no. 1: 291–318.

Stivers, Richard. 1999. *Technology as Magic: The Triumph of the Irrational*. New York: Continuum Publishing Company.

Stocker, Thomas F. and Dahe Qin. 2013. "Climate Change 2013: The Physical Science Basis." *IPCC Fifth Climate Assessment Report*. http://www.climat-echange2013.org/images/report/WG1AR5_ALL_FINAL.pdf

Stoll, Mark R. 2006. "Creating Ecology: Protestants and the Moral Community of Creation." In *Religion and the New Ecology*, edited by Lodge, David M. and Christopher Hamlin, 53–72. Notre Dame: University of Notre Dame Press.

Stoll, Mark R. 2015. *Inherit the Holy Mountain: Religion and the Rise of American Environmentalism*. New York: Oxford University Press.

Szrot, Lukas. 2015. *The Idols of Modernity: The Humanity of Science and the Science of Humanity*. M.A. Thesis, University of Texas at Arlington. Research Commons URI: http://hdl.handle.net/10106/25014

Szrot, Lukas. 2019. *America versus the Environment? Humanity, Nature, and the Sacred 1973–2014*. PhD diss., University of Kansas.

Szrot, Lukas. 2019a. ""Hamlet's Father: Hauntology and the Roots of the Modern Self." *Fast Capitalism* 16, no. 2: 87–94. https://fastcapitalism.journal.library.uta .edu/index.php/fastcapitalism/article/view/54

Szrot, Lukas. 2019b. "Lynn White, Reconsidered: Religiosity and Environmental Concern in the United States." *Journal of Behavioral and Social Sciences* 6, no. 1: 55–69.

Szrot, Lukas. 2020a. "From Stewardship to Creation Spirituality: The Evolving Ecological Ethos of Catholic Doctrine." *Journal for the Study of Religion, Nature, and Culture* 14, no. 2: 226–49. https://doi.org/10.1558/jsrnc.38023

Szrot, Lukas. 2020b. "From the Middle: Sites of Culture, Cooperation, and Trust in Risk Society." *This View of Life*, Special Issue. https://thisviewoflife.com/from-the -middle-sites-of-culture-cooperation-and-trust-in-risk-society/

Szrot, Lukas and Nathan R. Collins. 2019. "'Social Cocoons' Revisited: Examining the Correlates of Strict Religiosity via Encapsulation Theory." *Journal of Behavioral and Social Sciences* 6, no. 4: 219–31.

Taylor, Charles. 2007. *A Secular Age*. Cambridge: The Belknap Press of Harvard University Press.

Truelove, Heather Barnes and Jeff Joireman. 2009. "Understanding the Relationship between Christian Orthodoxy and Environmentalism: The Mediating Role of Perceived Environmental Consequences." *Environment and Behavior* 41, no. 6: 806–20.

Tucker, Mary Evelyn and John Grim. 2016. "Integrating Ecology and Justice: The Papal Encyclical." *The Quarterly Review of Biology* 91, no. 3: 261–70.

Vaidyanathan, Brandon, Simranjit Khalsa and Elaine Howard Ecklund. 2018. "Naturally Ambivalent: Religion's Role in Shaping Environmental Action." *Sociology of Religion* 79, no. 4: 472–94.

Vaisey, Stephen and Omar Lizardo. 2016. "Cultural Fragmentation or Acquired Dispositions? A New Approach to Accounting for Patterns of Cultural Change." *Socius* 2: 1–15.

Vidal, John. 2012. "Rio+20: Earth Summit Dawns with Stormier Clouds than in 1992." *The Guardian*, June 19, 2012. https://www.theguardian.com/environment /2012/jun/19/rio-20-earth-summit-1992-2012

Wade, Lisa and Myra Marx Ferree. 2019. *Gender: Ideas, Interactions, Institutions*. New York: W.W. Norton & Company.

Warner, R. Stephen and Rhys H. Williams. 2010. "The Role of Families and Religious Institutions in Transmitting Faith among Christians, Muslims, and Hindus in the USA." In *Religion and Youth*, edited by Sylvia Collins-Mayo and Pink Dandelion, 159–65. London: Ashgate.

Weber, Max. 1946. *From Max Weber: Essays in Sociology*. Translated, edited, and with an introduction by H.H. Gerth and C. Wright Mills. New York: Oxford University Press.

Weber, Max. 2011. *The Protestant Ethic and the Spirit of Capitalism*. Translated by Stephen Kalberg. New York: Oxford University Press.

White, Lynn, Jr. 1967. "The Historical Roots of Our Ecological Crisis." *Science* 155 (3767): 1203–07.

White, Richard. 1996. "'Are You an Environmentalist or Do You Work for a Living?': Work and Nature." *Uncommon Ground: Rethinking the Human Place in Nature*, edited by W. Cronon, 171–85. New York: Norton.

Whitney, Elspeth. 1993. "Lynn White, Ecotheology, and History." *Environmental Ethics* 15: 151–69.

Wilson, Edward O. 1998. *Consilience: The Unity of Knowledge*. New York: Knopf.

Wilson, Edward O. 2006. *The Creation: An Appeal to Save Life on Earth*. New York: W.W. Norton & Company.

Wilson, Edward O. 2016. *Half-Earth: Our Planet's Fight for Life*. New York: Liveright Publishing Corporation.

Wright, Erik Olin. 2015. "Sociological Limitations of the Climate Change Encyclical." *Nature Climate Change* 5, no. 10. https://doi.org/10.1038/nclimate2797

Wright, T.R. 1986. *The Religion of Humanity: The Impact of Comtean Positivism on Victorian Britain*. Cambridge: Cambridge University Press.

Yaple, Charles. 1982. *The Christian Church and Environmental Education: A Study of Involvements in the United States*. Ph.D. diss., State University of New York, Syracuse.

York, Richard and Eugene A. Rosa. 2003. "Key Challenges to Ecological Modernization Theory Institutional Efficacy, Case Study Evidence, Units of Analysis, and the Pace of Eco-Efficiency." *Organization & Environment* 16, no. 3: 273–88.

Zuckerman, Phil. 2012. *Faith No More: Why People Reject Religion*. New York: Oxford University Press.

Zuckerman, Phil. 2014. *Living the Secular Life: New Answers to Old Questions*. New York: Penguin Press.

Index

About the Author

Lukas Szrot is an assistant professor of sociology at Bemidji State University. His recent research has focused on the connection between religion and the environment in the U.S., with an emphasis on measuring how environmental attitudes have changed over time. Szrot has also written on the history of science, secularism, the social context of belief, public sociology, critical theory, the moral dimensions of human interaction, the connection between human beings and nature, and methodology in the social sciences. He has taught courses in theory, gender, research methods, social inequality, statistics, education, religion, politics, social movements, and social issues.